4 5-0

The Killing of Sister George

THE

KILLING OF

SISTER GEORGE

A Comedy by

Frank Marcus

 Random House · New York

FIRST AMERICAN PRINTING

© Copyright, 1965, by Frank Marcus

Library of Congress Catalog Card Number: 67-12758

Manufactured in the United States of America
by the Haddon Craftsmen, Scranton, Pennsylvania

C × H

THE KILLING OF SISTER GEORGE *was first presented by the Bristol Old Vic at the Theatre Royal, Bristol, by arrangement with Michael Codron. It was subsequently presented at the Duke of York's Theatre, London, on June 17th, 1965, by Michael Codron in association with Bernard Delfont with the following cast:*

(*In order of appearance*)

ALICE "CHILDIE" MCNAUGHT	Eileen Atkins
JUNE BUCKRIDGE (SISTER GEORGE)	Beryl Reid
MRS. MERCY CROFT	Lally Bowers
MADAME XENIA	Margaret Courtenay

It was first presented in the United States on October 5th, 1966, at the Belasco Theatre, New York, N.Y., by Helen Bonfils and Morton Gottlieb, by arrangement with Michael Codron in association with Bernard Delfont, with the original cast, except for Madame Xenia played by Polly Rowles.

Foreign Production designed by Catherine Browne
American Production supervised by William Ritman
Directed by Val May

SYNOPSIS OF SCENES

SCENE: The living room of June Buckridge's flat in Devonshire Street, London.

ACT ONE
An afternoon in late September.

ACT TWO
SCENE 1: A week later.
SCENE 2: The same day, evening.

ACT THREE
Two weeks later, morning.

Act One

The living room of a West End flat in London. A bay window at the back overlooks roofs. The furniture, an incongruous mixture of antique, nineteen-thirtyish, and modern, looks expensive but ill-assorted. There is a large radio, bearing trophies and framed certificates; elsewhere there are embroidered cushions in profusion, various bric-a-brac, and Victorian dolls are on the chairs and in the corner of a chintz-covered settee. Downstage right an arch leads to the hall and entrance; upstage left a door leads to the bedroom; a passage off up left leads to the bathroom, and another door downstage leads to the kitchen. The Curtain rises on an empty stage. It is a Tuesday afternoon in late September. Presently the front door bangs, and JUNE BUCKRIDGE *enters. She is a rotund, middle-aged woman, wearing a belted white mackintosh. She is very agitated.*

ALICE (*Calling from the kitchen*) George? . . . George, is that you? (JUNE *opens a cigar box, finds it empty and throws it down.* ALICE *throws up the hatch between the kitchen and the living room.* ALICE *is a girl-woman in her thirties, looking deceptively young. She conveys an impression of pallor: her hair, eyes and complexion are all very light. She is wearing a sweater and jeans, with a plastic apron and orange rubber gloves, having been in the middle of the washing up. She is very surprised.*) George, what on earth . . . ?

(JUNE *throws a doll on the floor*) George, what are you doing at home at this time of the afternoon?
(JUNE *lights a cheroot from a box on the mantelpiece*)

3

JUNE (*After a pause*) They are going to murder me.

ALICE What—

JUNE I've suspected it for some time.

ALICE What?

JUNE Will you kindly close that hatch?

ALICE (*Closing the hatch and entering the sitting room from the kitchen*) What are you talking about?

JUNE (*Brutally*) Shut up. You know nothing. (ALICE, *silenced, watches* JUNE *puffing nervously on her cigar*) That Australian bitch, that Sheila, let it out . . .

ALICE The one who used to be a lady cricketer?

JUNE (*With disgust*) Yes—the lolloping great trollop!

ALICE So, what did she say?

JUNE (*Very excited now*) It was in the tea-break, when she gave me a cup of tea. "I trust you're in good health," she said, with a sly wink.

ALICE There's nothing wrong with that.

JUNE I knew what she meant. I got the message.

ALICE It might have been quite innocuous—

JUNE Innocuous! They are trying to kill me, and you call that innocuous! (*Pacing up and down*) Somebody's leaked it to her—another Australian. They're everywhere: the place is rampant with them; they multiply like rabbits.

ALICE You're imagining things.

JUNE No not rabbits, opossums!! Dreary little pests.

ALICE Well, anyway, what did you *do*?

JUNE I left.

ALICE (*Alarmed*) You walked out of rehearsal?

JUNE (*Subdued*) I wasn't going to let some illiterate bitch wink at me . . .

ALICE (*Biting her lip*) They won't like it . . .

JUNE I've given six years' devoted service to that program.

ALICE You said yourself: they don't like contract artists to have tantrums—

JUNE (*Getting excited again*) They have no right to do this to me. I'm a senior member of the cast. If they wanted to—(*She swallows*) write me out, they should have called me to the office in the proper manner—

ALICE Nobody wants to write you out. It's unthinkable. Applehurst couldn't survive without you . . .

JUNE Don't you be too sure. Applehurst is more than a village, you know—it's a community, a way of life. It doesn't depend on individuals. There's many a stone in that churchyard . . .

ALICE You talk as if it was real—

JUNE (*Raising her voice again*) It's real to millions! It stands for the traditional values of English life—tenacity —common sense—our rural heritage—

ALICE Oh, belt up.

JUNE You're getting above yourself, Missy.

ALICE But you *are* the serial! It would be nothing without you—

JUNE Stranger things have happened. Only the other day Ronnie said: "There'll have to be some changes, you know."

ALICE He probably meant the story line—

JUNE No—no—it's the axe again! We're losing listeners, and they've got to have a scapegoat. It's over a year since old Mrs. Prescott was kicked by a horse . . .

ALICE Yes, and remember the rumpus there was over that! And she was only a minor character—

JUNE She had her following.

ALICE She hardly had a line to say from one week to the next.

JUNE What about the time I nursed her back to health, when she had concussion?

ALICE That was exceptional.

JUNE No, no, no. She had nice little bits—here and there. Remember that time she found the stray dog, and the village adopted it—(*A dark thought occurs to her*)— until it was run over by a tractor.
(*She shudders*)

ALICE There is no comparison. Mrs. Prescott—

JUNE (*Shouting*) Mrs. Prescott had a following.

ALICE (*Shrugging her shoulders*) All right: Mrs. Prescott had a following.

6

JUNE   The subject is now closed.
(*Pause*)

ALICE   But she *was* expendable.

JUNE (*Exploding*)   Are you trying to aggravate me? Are
you deliberately trying to annoy me?

ALICE   You're the most popular character in it—

JUNE   Don't screech at me. It's an ugly, grating sound.

ALICE   Well, look at your ratings.

JUNE   They are down! Four per cent last week—I'm slipping! Now do you understand?
(*Pause*)

ALICE   You still get the most fan mail, don't you?

JUNE   Only just . . . Ginger, the pubkeeper, is close on
my heels. Ever since he had that win on the Premium
Bonds, and lent the money to Farmer Bromley, so as they
wouldn't turn his place into a factory farm—

ALICE   What about young Rosie?

JUNE (*Conspiratorially*)   Aha. (ALICE *looks   puzzled*)
She's preggers.

ALICE   No! You mean the actress—

JUNE   No, the character, blockhead! We reckon that'll
bring back some listeners.

ALICE (*Intrigued*)   Who was responsible?

JUNE   We haven't been told yet. I think it was Lennie,

7

her steady. If so, it'll be absolutely splendid. They can get married—everybody loves a wedding. But Arthur thinks it was Roy.

ALICE   Who's Roy?

JUNE   That soldier—from the army camp at Oakmead. He took her to that dance, remember?

ALICE (*Concerned*)   What's she going to do . . . about the baby?

JUNE   She's going to confide in me about it—in the next installment. Comes to me in tears; wants to get rid of it . . . (*Sighing*) Don't know what the younger generation's coming to . . .

ALICE   What do you tell her?

JUNE   What *don't* I tell her! She gets a dressing-down from me that she won't forget in a hurry! (*In her country accent*) Where is he? Mr. Clever Lad? Show me where he is, so's I can tear some strips off him, the fine young fellow. Just don't you aggravate yourself, my dear—leave it to me! My dear, who was it? Just tell me who it was!

ALICE   And does she tell you?

JUNE   No. (*Pause*) But I'll wheedle it out of her, never fear. Give me three installments and I'll do it.

ALICE (*Tensely*)   They shouldn't talk about . . . things like that.

JUNE (*Happier now*)   It's nice, though, the way they come to me . . . with their troubles . . . Oh, they know they'll get straight talking from me—no lard ever passed my lips. No, sir, fine words butter no parsnips.

ALICE   What the hell are you on about?

JUNE   They *need* me. Get that into your thick head: Applehurst needs a District Nurse. Who'd deliver the babies, who'd look after the old folk, I'd like to know?!

ALICE   Exactly! Nobody's suggesting—

JUNE   What do you mean, nobody's suggesting? Why did that woman ask about my health, then? Why did she wink at me, eh?

ALICE   Perhaps she fancies you.

JUNE   This is no time for jesting.

ALICE   How am I to know why she winked at you. Perhaps she has a nervous twitch?

JUNE   She's Australian, dunce! They're extroverts, not neurotic townsfolk like us. They come from the bloody bush!

ALICE   (*Becoming exasperated*)   Well, I don't know why she winked at you!

JUNE   Oh, shut up! Stupid bitch. (*She goes to the radio and reads out one of the framed certificates*) "And in recognition of your devoted work and care for the old and sick, we name the Geriatric Ward the Sister George Ward." (ALICE *applauds slowly and ironically*) Take care, Childie, you're trailing your coat . . .

ALICE   (*Giggling*)   You're the bull . . .

9

JUNE (*Dangerously*) We're very cocky all of a sudden!

ALICE (*Mock-innocently*) Who, me?

JUNE Yes, you. Anyway, what the hell are you doing at home on a Tuesday afternoon? Why aren't you at work?

ALICE Mr. Katz gave us the day off. It's a Jewish holiday.

JUNE (*Suspiciously*) Oh, really. What holiday?

ALICE I don't know. The Feast of the Contamination, or something.

JUNE You seem to have more holidays than workdays just lately.

ALICE Not my fault.

JUNE (*Still suspicious*) He hasn't "had a go" at you again, your Mr. Katz, has he?

ALICE (*Primly*) Certainly not.

JUNE I bet he has.

ALICE He hasn't. I'd tell you.

JUNE I wonder. (*Self-pityingly*) Nobody tells me anything.

ALICE That's because you always make a stupid fuss about things.

JUNE All right, I won't make a fuss. Go on, tell me.

ALICE There's nothing to tell.

JUNE (*Venomously*) You expect me to believe that! After what happened last time?

ALICE   Nothing happened!

JUNE   Oh, no? A four-inch tear and three buttons off your blouse—you call that nothing?

ALICE   I told you. I got it caught in the Xerox.

JUNE   Don't lie to me, Childie.

ALICE   I'm not lying.

JUNE   Why do you avoid my eyes, then?

ALICE   Because . . . because—Oh! You're impossible, George.
　　　(*She runs off into the bathroom*)

JUNE   Don't throw tantrums with me, young lady. (*Roaring*) Come out! Come out this instant!

ALICE (*From the bathroom*)   I shan't.

JUNE (*Picking up one of the Victorian dolls*)   Can you hear me, Childie? I've got Emmeline here, your favorite doll. (*Softly, but clearly*) And if you don't come out of the bathroom AT ONCE . . . I'll pull Emmeline's head off . . .

ALICE (*Tear-stained, rushes into the room, tears the doll out of* JUNE's *hands, and hugs it*)   Monster . . .

JUNE   There, that's better. (*Pause*) And now: apologize.

ALICE   What for?

JUNE   For causing me unnecessary aggravation.

ALICE   I'm sorry.

JUNE   You don't sound it.

11

ALICE   Look, I know that you're worried and everything, but that's no reason—

JUNE   Don't answer back. Don't be cheeky.

ALICE   Look, George—

JUNE   Has Mr. Katz "had a go" at you?

ALICE (*Screaming*)   No ! ! !

JUNE   Don't screech at me! Apologize this instant, or there'll be severe chastisement.

ALICE   I'm sorry.

JUNE   That's better. Now—down on your knees.

ALICE   Must I?

JUNE   Yes. (ALICE, *still hugging the doll, goes on her knees*) Come on—show your contrition.

ALICE   How?

JUNE (*Pointing to the ashtray*)   Eat the butt of my cigar.

ALICE   I couldn't: it would make me sick.

JUNE (*Standing over* ALICE)   Are you arguing with me?

ALICE   O.K. Hand it over.

JUNE   Good girl. Now eat it.

ALICE   Can I take the ash off?

JUNE   You may take the ash off, but you must eat the paper.

(*With an expression of extreme distaste,* ALICE *eats the cigar butt*)

ALICE   It tastes vile.

JUNE   Good. That'll teach you to be rude.
(*The telephone rings*)

ALICE (*Rushing to answer it, relieved to be let off her punishment*)   Hello, yes, this is Miss June Buckridge's flat.
One moment, please.

JUNE (*Apprehensive*)   Who is it?

ALICE   I don't know.

JUNE   Why didn't you ask, fathead? (*She takes the receiver*) Hello, this is Miss June Buckridge . . . Who
wants her? Yes, of course . . . Yes, I'll hold on . . . (*Putting her hand over the mouthpiece*) God Almighty,
Childie, it's the BBC.

ALICE (*Trembling*)   O Lord, I hope it's nothing serious . . .

JUNE (*On the telephone*)   Hello? Hello, Mrs. Mercy,
dear . . . No, of *course* not . . . Quite . . . Quite. Oh,
I'm *feeling* all right . . . Yes, I . . . Well, as a matter
of fact, there *is* something . . . Perhaps we'd better
have a man-to-man—You have something to say to *me*?
No, I'm not doing anything at the moment . . . Well,
I'd rather not come back to BH today . . . Yes, yes,
that's a *splendid* idea! Love to see you! That's right:
Devonshire Street . . . top floor. You press the bell, and
one of those "I speak your weight" machines answers
—(*A rather forced laugh*) Yes, you know the kind of
thing—(*Intoning in a deep voice*) "You are thirteen stone
ten" —No, no, of course not—I wasn't implying . . . Yes,
that'll be lovely . . . *any* time . . . 'Bye. (*She hangs up,*

13

wipes her brow) She's coming round. (*Nervously lighting another cheroot*) She'll be here in a minute. God, I'm for it!

ALICE   Who was it?

JUNE   The Assistant Head . . . Mrs. Mercy Croft—

ALICE   The one who has that weekly spot on Woman's Hour?

JUNE   "Ask Mrs. Mercy"—that's her!

ALICE   But she sounds awfully nice on the radio—at least, her advice is sort of . . . sensible.

JUNE   She is nice . . . (*Trying to convince herself*) Mrs. Mercy is a *nice woman*.

ALICE   Well, then.

JUNE   She's coming to me, you understand? At first, she asked me to see her in her office . . .

ALICE (*After a pause*)   Did she seem friendly?

JUNE (*Tensely*)   Yep.

ALICE   It'll be a good thing to clear the air—

JUNE   You don't know what you're talking about! She wants to see me on an urgent matter. We must brace ourselves for the worst—

ALICE   Will she expect some tea?

JUNE   Tea, yes of course. You must make her something special—at the double.

ALICE There's that piece of Dundee cake that mother sent—

JUNE That'll be absolutely first class. And make her some of your Scotch scones! And when you're serving, look cheerful, keep your shoulders back, try to make a good impression. And if she speaks to you don't open your mouth about things you don't understand.

ALICE I can quite easily go out.

JUNE What, and leave me to pour tea and all that pansy stuff? Not likely. You'll stay here and do some work.

ALICE Look, George. Try not to show how worried you are. You always get sort of . . . aggressive when you're nervous.

JUNE Go on. Back to the kitchen where you belong!

ALICE I wish you'd do relaxing exercises, or something. (*Exits*)

JUNE (*Shouting after her*) I'll do relaxing exercises on your behind, if you're not careful! Now then. (*She goes to arrange the display on the radio*) "Personality of the Year"—I'll put that in a prominent position . . . The English Village Preservation Society . . . The Association of British Nursing Sisters . . . the Variety Club of Great Britain . . . "Miss Humanity" nominated by the *Daily Mirror* . . . There's something missing . . . (*Calling*) Alice!

ALICE (*From the kitchen*) I'm busy!

JUNE (*Imperiously*) Come here! I want you.

ALICE (*Re-entering*) What is it NOW? You're always interrupting . . .

JUNE There's one missing.
(*She points to the trophies*)

ALICE I haven't touched anything—

JUNE There's one missing, isn't there? Go on—*have a look!* I want to hear you tell me, in your own words, which one is missing.

ALICE (*Without looking*) I don't know.

JUNE (*Softly, with deadly emphasis*) Where's the Honorary "Stag"?

ALICE (*Uncertainly*) What—

JUNE (*As before*) What have you done with it? (*No reply from* ALICE) I give you ten seconds to confess. (*She waits, breathing heavily*)

ALICE Let me get on with the tea. She'll be here in a minute . . .

JUNE You've destroyed it, haven't you? (*Pause*) Where is the Honorary "Stag"?

ALICE I threw it away.

JUNE You . . . *what?*

ALICE (*Slightly hysterically*) I *hated* it! A cut-off stag's head. Impaled on a pike! You had no right to keep such abominations in the house—you know I like animals!

JUNE When did you throw it away?

ALICE Last night.
(*She has started to cry, silently*)

JUNE It meant a lot to me—being elected an Honorary "Stag" . . .

16

ALICE (*Very contrite now*) I'll get it back; I'll get another.

JUNE (*Tragically*) Too late.

ALICE I'll telephone to the Town Hall—the Borough Litter Disposal Unit—

JUNE (*Still tragically*) You mean the dustmen, don't you . . . why can't you bloody well say so . . . (*The buzzer rings*) It's her: the bitch, the cow, the plague spot, the embossed carbuncle—(JUNE *answers the buzzer*) Hello, Mrs. Mercy, dear. Expecting you. Yes, top floor. (*She switches off*) Don't stand about gawping! Blow your nose. Pull your sweater straight: you look disgusting. Now, remember: be polite and keep mum. I'll speak to you later. (*Pause*) Where the hell has she got to?

ALICE Maybe she got stuck in the lift.

JUNE (*Aghast*) The lift door! I think I forgot to close the door.

ALICE (*Rushing to the door*) I'll do it!

JUNE (*In a hoarse whisper*) Don't—it's too late! She'll either walk, or . . .
 (*The doorbell rings*)

ALICE (*Suddenly scared*) Let's not open the door!
 (JUNE *throws* ALICE *a glance expressing contempt, and strides out to open the door*)

JUNE (*Offstage*) Oh hello, Mrs. Mercy! I'm so sorry— I'd only just remembered that the lift was out of order . . .

MRS. MERCY (*Entering, cheerfully*) Not at all—I never use the lift. (*Seeing* ALICE) Oh?
 (MRS. MERCY *is a well-groomed lady of indeterminate age, gracious of manner, and freezingly polite.*

17

She is wearing a gray two-piece suit, matching hat and accessories, and a discreet double string of pearls round her neck. She carries a briefcase)

JUNE May I introduce—Miss Alice McNaught, Mrs. Croft.

MRS. MERCY *(Extending her hand)* How do you do? *(Turning to* JUNE*)* Yes, I always say: we get far too little exercise these days. If we walked the stairs, instead of using lifts, those extra inches would disappear.

ALICE *(Trying to be helpful)* I sometimes walk—

MRS. MERCY You don't need to lose any weight, my dear—

JUNE Alice is just preparing the tea—

MRS. MERCY Oh, that is nice. I do hope I haven't put you to any trouble—inviting myself out of the blue.

JUNE Rubbish.

ALICE Not at all.
       *(*ALICE *goes to the kitchen)*

MRS. MERCY May I look around? I ADORE looking at other people's flats—they do reflect their occupier's personalities in an uncannily accurate way. *(Looking round)* To be perfectly honest, I imagined your home to be . . . different.

JUNE Really?

MRS. MERCY This charming Victoriana . . . the dolls . . . Somehow—

JUNE *(Slightly embarrassed)* They're Miss McNaught's.

18

MRS. MERCY   Oh, of course, that would explain it. They just weren't *you*. I didn't know—

JUNE   (*Rather sheepishly*)   Yes, I have a flatmate . . .

MRS. MERCY (*Sympathetically*)   How nice. It's so important to have . . . companionship—especially when one's an artist . . .

JUNE   These are mine—I collect horse brasses.

MRS. MERCY   How useful . . . May I look out from your window? I love overlooking things. I've always adored heights; in my young days, my husband and I often used to go mountaineering—in the Austrian Alps for preference. (*She has gone to the window*) Oh! (*A sudden yell of delight*) There's BH! You can see Broadcasting House from your window—isn't that . . . *super!* To have that reassuring presence brooding over you, seeing that you don't get into mischief!

ALICE   (*Lifting the hatch and looking into the room*) Ready in a minute.

MRS. MERCY   Oh—good!

JUNE   Would you kindly close the hatch. (ALICE *shuts the hatch*) There are times when I have an almost irresistible urge to decapitate her.

MRS. MERCY   Oh, poor Miss McNaught. I do like your settee cover—a homely pattern. I love floral design—I know it's old-fashioned, but . . .

JUNE   Childie—Miss McNaught—made them.

MRS. MERCY   Really. How clever of her—they're beautifully fitted. You're fortunate to have such a handy companion.

19

JUNE (*With a bitter look at the trophies*) Yes, she's good with the needle, I'll say that for her.

MRS. MERCY (*Lightly*) That was Sister George speaking.

JUNE (*Self-consciously*) One can't help slipping—

MRS. MERCY But you *are* Sister George far more than Miss June Buckridge to all of us at BH.

JUNE Jolly nice of you to say so.
(*Motions her to sit*)

MRS. MERCY Thank you. You have made the part completely your own—it was obvious—even at the first auditions. I remember it quite clearly, although it must be, oh—

JUNE Almost six years ago. I was scared stiff, too.

MRS. MERCY How charming! One can't imagine you scared stiff!

JUNE I don't mind physical danger, I even like it. I manned an anti-aircraft during the war.

MRS. MERCY Lovely!

JUNE None of that sissy troop entertainment for yours truly!

MRS. MERCY It wasn't that bad. As a matter of fact, I did a bit of organizing for ENSA myself . . .

JUNE I'm sorry. No offense meant.

MRS. MERCY None taken. Now Miss Buckridge—or may I call you Sister George, like everybody else?

JUNE Certainly.

MRS. MERCY As you know I hold a monthly Surgery in my office, when I welcome people to come to me with their problems. I've always made it a rule to be approachable. In some cases, involving matters of special importance, I prefer to visit the subjects in their own homes, so that we can talk more easily without any duress. That's why I'm here today.

JUNE (*In her country accent*) Ah well, farmer's footsteps are the best manure!

MRS. MERCY Quite. There's rather a serious matter I wish to discuss with you.

ALICE (*Entering with tea*) Sorry I took so long.

MRS. MERCY Ah, *lovely!* (*To* JUNE) We'll continue our little chat after tea.

ALICE If you'd rather—

JUNE You can speak quite freely, Mrs. Mercy. Miss McNaught and I have no secrets from each other.

MRS. MERCY Well, let's all have tea first . . .(*As* ALICE *lays the table*) I say, what delicious-looking scones!

ALICE They're Scotch scones.

JUNE They're Childie's speciality. Copied from her grandmother's recipe.

MRS. MERCY They look delish! May I try one?

ALICE Help yourself. Here's the jam.

MRS. MERCY They're what we used to call Girdle Scones—

JUNE   Or Drop Scones—

ALICE   It's important not to get the girdle too hot, or the outside of the scones will brown before the inside is cooked.

MRS. MERCY   They're a lovely even color . . .

ALICE   (*Very animated*)   I always cool them in a towel—

MRS. MERCY   Do you?

ALICE   Yes, and I wait till the bubbles rise to the surface before I turn them over—

MRS. MERCY   They're very successful.

ALICE   I use half a teaspoon of bicarbonate of soda—

MRS. MERCY   Now you're giving away trade secrets.

ALICE   And one level teaspoon of cream of tartar—

JUNE   (*Rising*)   Shut up!
         (*There is a moment's silence*)

ALICE   Eight ounces of flour—

JUNE   (*Exploding*)   Shut up!

ALICE   (*Softly*)   And one egg.

JUNE   Shut up! !
         (JUNE *hurls a cake in* ALICE'S *direction*)

MRS. MERCY   (*Continuing to eat, unperturbed*)   Now then, girls—temper!

ALICE   She hates me to talk about food. (*Confidentially to* MRS. MERCY)   She's a wee bit overwrought—

JUNE   Overwrought, my arse!

ALICE (*Chiding*)   Now that wasn't nice— that was not a nice thing to say.

MRS. MERCY (*Smiling indulgently*)   I expect she picked it up in the army.

ALICE   She swears like a trooper—

MRS. MERCY   But she has a heart of gold.

ALICE   One day, she got into such a temper, I wrote a poem about it.

JUNE (*Bitterly*)   Yes, she fancies herself as a poetess. Goes to the City Lit. every Wednesday night, to learn about metre and things—

MRS. MERCY   What a nice hobby.

JUNE   As a poetess, she makes a good cook.

MRS. MERCY   It's still a question of mixing the right ingredients to make a tasty whole.

ALICE   That night she came back in a raging temper—

JUNE   Thank you very much, we don't want to hear anything about that—

ALICE   I wrote this poem. It began:
   "Fierce as the wind
   Blows the rampaging termagent . . ."

MRS. MERCY   Very expressive. (*To* JUNE) And how did you like being compared to the wind?
   (JUNE *blows a raspberry*)

23

ALICE (*To* MRS. MERCY) Slice of cake, Mrs. Mercy?

MRS. MERCY Just a teeny one. Mustn't be greedy.

JUNE Her mother made it.

MRS. MERCY You can always tell if it's home-baked; it tastes quite different.

JUNE You'd be surprised if you knew what Mother McNaught put into it.

MRS. MERCY I'm not even going to ask.

JUNE I'm delighted to hear it!
(*Laughs*)

MRS. MERCY (*Enjoying herself*) Oh dear, this is just like a dormitory feast—all this girlish banter. (*To* JUNE) I bet you were a terror at school!

JUNE I was captain of the hockey team and a keen disciplinarian—God help the girl I caught making me an apple-pie bed!
(*She chuckles*)

MRS. MERCY Ah, there's Sister George again! It's wonderful how over the years the character *evolved* . . .

ALICE Who first thought of putting her on a motorbike?

JUNE That was because of sound effects. As long as I was on the old bike, listeners never knew whether I was static or mobile.

MRS. MERCY A unique sound—Sister George on her motorbike, whizzing through the countryside, singing snatches of hymns—

JUNE One day I got into trouble because I sang a hymn which sounded like "On the Good Ship Venus."

MRS. MERCY   A traditional air—?

JUNE   I've found it safer to stick to hymns. Once I tried a pop song, and d'you know, hundreds of letters came in, protesting.

MRS. MERCY   We learn from experience . . . But we don't want Applehurst falling behind the times.

JUNE   No—no—of course not.

MRS. MERCY   But we must constantly examine criticism, and if it's constructive, we must act on it. Ruthlessly.

JUNE   What sort of criticism?

MRS. MERCY   Oh, nothing in particular . . . at least . . .

JUNE   But what?

MRS. MERCY   Well, that brings me—I'm afraid—to the unpleasant part of my business . . .

ALICE   Oh dear—

MRS. MERCY   (Rising)   But first, would you show me to the little girls' room?

JUNE   Alice, show Mrs. Mercy to the . . .

ALICE   This way, Mrs. Mercy.

JUNE   —little—girls'—

> (MRS. MERCY exits, accompanied by ALICE. JUNE catches sight of her briefcase, looks round furtively, and opens it as ALICE returns)

ALICE   (Aghast)   What are you doing?

25

JUNE (*Rummaging in the case*) Keep a look-out!

ALICE You can't. You mustn't!

JUNE (*Taking a folder*) My personal file.

ALICE (*In a hysterical whisper*) PUT IT BACK!

JUNE (*Perusing some papers*) Quiet! (*She takes an envelope from the file. Reads*) "Sister George. Confidential."

ALICE She's coming!

JUNE (*Quickly replaces the folder in the briefcase, realizes too late that she has still got the envelope in her hand: puts it behind the nearest cushion*) ... so Emmeline said, "I don't want any Girdle Scones ... thank you very much."

MRS. MERCY (*Re-entering*) I got on the scales, to see if I've put on any weight.

JUNE I don't suppose ...

MRS. MERCY (*Takes her briefcase, while* JUNE *and* ALICE *stand rigid with suspense*) Now then ...

ALICE I'll make myself scarce ...
(*Goes into kitchen*)

MRS. MERCY Please sit down. (JUNE *sits*) You won't hold it against me if I speak quite plainly?

JUNE Please do.

MRS. MERCY It's my unpleasant duty to haul you over the coals, and administer a severe reprimand.

JUNE Oh?

MRS. MERCY Believe me, Sister George, I'd much rather let bygones be bygones—

JUNE (*In a country accent*) Let sleeping dogs lie—

MRS. MERCY Precisely . . . But I must remind you of the little chat we had just about a year ago, after that unfortunate incident in the Club . . . involving a lady colleague of mine.

JUNE Let's not rake over old embers.

MRS. MERCY I don't intend to. But in the light of recent events, it's difficult to forget an incident as vivid as the pouring of a glass of beer over the Assistant Head of Talks. I had hoped one black mark would have been enough for you, but this morning (*Takes a sheet of paper from the folder*) I received this memo from the Director of Religious Broadcasting. (*She hands the paper to* JUNE) I should like to have your comments.

JUNE (*Excitedly reads the paper, flushes, and jumps up violently*) It's a lie! It's an utter, bloody lie!

MRS. MERCY (*Firmly*) Please calm yourself, Miss Buckridge. Kindly hand me back the paper.

JUNE (*Handing over the paper*) I take it you're not denying that you were drinking in The Coach & Horses on the night of the nineteenth?

JUNE How the hell should I remember? (*Calling*) Alice! Come here!

ALICE (*Enters, wide-eyed and worried*) You want me?

JUNE Where was I on the night of the nineteenth?

27

MRS. MERCY I'm sorry to involve you in this, Miss Mc-
Naught—

ALICE (*Quietly*) That was a Wednesday: I was at the
City Lit.

JUNE You bloody well would be. (*To* MRS. MERCY) All
right; it seems I was at The Coach & Horses on the night
in question, having a drink with some of the boys. That's
no crime.

MRS. MERCY Miss Buckridge . . . According to this letter
from the Mother Superior of the Convent of the Sacred
Heart of Jesus, you boarded a taxi stopping at the traffic
lights at Langham Place—

JUNE I thought it was empty.

MRS. MERCY (*Reading*) A taxi bearing as passengers two
novitiate nuns from Ireland who had just arrived at Kings
Cross Station—

JUNE How was I to know?

MRS. MERCY You boarded this taxi in a state of advanced
inebriation and—(*Consulting the paper*)—proceeded to
assault the two nuns, subjecting them to actual physical
violence!

ALICE (*To* JUNE) You didn't really!

JUNE No, no, no. Of course not. I'd had a few pints . . .
I saw this cab, took it to be empty, got in—and there
were these two black things screaming blue murder!

MRS. MERCY Why didn't you get out again?

JUNE Well, I'd had a very nasty shock myself! What with their screaming and flapping about—I thought they were bats, you know, vampire bats! It was they who attacked me. I remember getting all entangled in their skirts and petticoats and things . . . the taxi driver had to pull me free . . .

MRS. MERCY A deplorable anecdote. According to the Mother Superior, one of the nuns required medical treatment for shock, and is still under sedation. She thought it was the devil.

ALICE George, how could you!

JUNE Don't you start on me! (*Clapping her hands*) Back to the kitchen! Washing up! Presto!

ALICE (*Firmly*) No, I'm staying. This concerns me, too.

JUNE It was all a ghastly mistake.

MRS. MERCY No doubt, but it'll take some explaining.

JUNE Fancy informing the Director of Religious Broadcasting. What a nasty thing to do for a holy woman!

MRS. MERCY The Mother Superior is responsible for the nuns in her charge—

JUNE Then she should jolly well teach them how to behave in public! I got the fright of my life, in there! Those nuns were like *mice*—albino mice—with white faces and little red eyes. And they were vicious, too. They scratched and they bit! Look—you can still see the tooth marks— (*She points to her arm*)—do you see that? I've a good mind to make a counter-complaint to the Mother Superior: they deserve to be scourged in their cells.

MRS. MERCY (*Wearily*) I can hardly put through a report to the Controller, informing him of your allegation that you were bitten by two nuns!

JUNE No, well, you could say—

MRS. MERCY Let's be practical, Sister George—we're concerned with retaining the trust and respect of the public. Now people understand perfectly well that artists frequently work under great emotional stress. We do all we can to gloss over the minor disciplinary offences. But we simply cannot tolerate this sort of behavior. It's things like this which make people resent paying more for their wireless licences! Thousands of pounds spent on public relations, and you jeopardize it all with your reckless and foolish actions. Really, Sister George, we have reason to be very, very angry with you.

JUNE (*Beaten*) What do you want me to do?

MRS. MERCY You must write a letter immediately to the Mother Superior. You must sincerely apologize for your behavior and I suggest you offer a small donation for some charity connected with the Convent. Then you must send a copy of your letter to the Director of Religious Broadcasting, with a covering note from you, couched in suitable terms.

JUNE You mean humbling myself.

ALICE Don't worry, Mrs. Mercy. I'll see she does it and I'll make quite sure she doesn't get into any mischief in the future.

MRS. MERCY There speaks a true friend. (*To* JUNE)

You're very lucky to have someone like Miss McNaught to rely on. Treasure her.

JUNE (*Bitterly*) I'll treasure her, all right!

ALICE I'll see to it that the letters are written and sent off right away!

MRS. MERCY (*Rising*) Good. That's what I like to hear. (*To* JUNE) I'll leave you in Miss McNaught's expert charge.

JUNE What about Applehurst?

MRS. MERCY (*Non-committally*) That's another, rather more complex problem . . .

JUNE But . . . has anything been decided about the future?

MRS. MERCY I'm afraid I can't say anything about that at the moment.

JUNE It comes as a bit of a shock to me, you know, all this.

MRS. MERCY It comes as a bit of a shock to me too, I assure you—especially as I understand that you often open church bazaars—

ALICE I'll look after her—I'll keep her away from convents.

MRS. MERCY You keep her on a tight rein, and all will be well.

ALICE Of course I will. Between us we'll keep her in order.

31

MRS. MERCY   She won't have a chance, will she?

JUNE   Look here—I'm sorry—you know—if I've been a bad boy.

MRS. MERCY (*Turning to* JUNE *and shaking hands*)   Well, good-bye, dear Sister George. Keep your chin up. Things are never as bad as they seem—

JUNE (*Listlessly, in her country accent*)   Every cloud has a silver lining . . .

MRS. MERCY   That's the spirit! And—(*Whispering confidentially*) No more walk-outs at rehearsals, eh? If you have any complaints do come and see me about them.

JUNE (*In her country accent*)   Well, it's the creaking gate that gets oiled . . .

MRS. MERCY (*Reflecting for a moment*)   A somewhat unfortunate simile . . . (*To* ALICE) So nice to have met you—

ALICE   Nice to have met *you*, Mrs. Mercy. What's the subject of your talk tomorrow? Is it a secret, or are you allowed to tell?

MRS. MERCY (*Smiling graciously*)   It's family planning this week—and foundation garments next!
(*She sails out, followed by* ALICE. JUNE *nervously lights a cheroot. There are sounds of conversation from outside, then the front door closes.* ALICE *returns and gives* JUNE *a meaningful look*)

ALICE   Well!

JUNE (*Alarmed*)   Did she say anything? Did she drop any hints behind my back?

ALICE   No. Just general comments—you know—about nuns in taxis.

JUNE   What do you mean?

ALICE   Nuns. You know, n-u-n-s. Brides of Christ.

JUNE   Oh, I see, that's what's biting you.

ALICE   (*In an outburst*)   How could you! How could you make such an exhibition of yourself!

JUNE   For heaven's sake, Childie, grow up. Don't be so bloody . . . *squeamish.*

ALICE   (*Primly*)   I think you owe me some sort of explanation.

JUNE   (*Chuckling*)   All those petticoats . . .

ALICE   It's the sort of thing you used to do when I first knew you. In that Club in Notting Hill Gate: I remember how you used to go clomping about, without a bra, hitting girls over the head.

JUNE   Kindly keep those foul-mouthed recollections to yourself. In my young days . . .

ALICE   Your young days were spent in a cul-de-sac in Aldershot, with the Band of Hope on one side and the foot clinic on the other. You told me so yourself.

JUNE   How dare you. This is a respectable house—and don't forget who's paying the rent!

ALICE   Not much longer, perhaps.

33

JUNE   They wouldn't dare get rid of me because of this
. . . of this trivial incident . . .

ALICE (*Imitating* JUNE's *country accent*)   We none of us
know what the future holds for us.

JUNE (*After a pause, puffing on her cigar*)   I'm worried. I
really am worried, Childie. Please, do me a favor . . .

ALICE   What?

JUNE   Go and ask Madame Xenia to come up. She's an
expert on the future.

ALICE   She's probably got a client—

JUNE   Maybe she's between appointments. Go on.

ALICE   I can't just barge in—

JUNE   Why not? You've done it before. Remember when
I was bitten by that Lakeland terrier and you thought I
had the rabies! She always knows what's going to happen. Go on.

ALICE   Oh.

JUNE   This is an emergency. Extreme measures must be
taken at once! Go and get her at once!

ALICE   I can't. She hates my guts.

JUNE   Madame Xenia? Why?

ALICE   She thinks I'm after her lodger. (JUNE *rises menacingly*) It's complete fantasy.

JUNE (*Ominously, in the voice of Sister George*)   There's
no smoke without fire!

34

ALICE Just like the last one you scared off.

JUNE I could see which way the wind was blowing. I nipped it in the bud.

ALICE I only helped him with his homework. He was a mere boy.

JUNE (*Decisively*) There's nothing mere about boys . . . Now go and fetch her at once and watch your step.

ALICE (*Going*) You've always got to have someone doing your dirty work.

JUNE Thanks, you're a pal. (ALICE *goes.* JUNE *reads the inscription on a frame on the table*) ". . . and for your devoted work and care for the old and sick."
(*Gets out the envelope from behind the cushion. Looks at it, puts it back*)

ALICE (*Off-stage*) I'm sorry to drag you away . . .

MADAME XENIA That's all right. I know. I know. George! (*Enter* MADAME XENIA, *a hawk-faced, elderly lady of foreign origin, henna-ed and hung with beads.* ALICE *follows*) George? Darling? What is the matter?

ALICE Madame was in the middle of a consultation with a client—

JUNE Oh, I *am* sorry.

XENIA Never mind. You are my friend. Always you come first. Now, darling, what's the trouble?

JUNE Madame Xenia, I'm worried out of my wits . . . it's the BBC. They're driving me mad—

35

XENIA They will suffer for it. I will put curses on them. (*Professionally*) Sit down; make yourself at home.

JUNE Thanks.

XENIA I forget; I always say it to people to make them relax. Right— (*To* JUNE) Would you draw the curtains, please?

JUNE (*Goes to draw the curtains*) Certainly.

XENIA (*To* ALICE) And you: will you please sit facing the East?

ALICE Which way's the East?

XENIA (*Pointing*) There. Towards Great Portland Street.

ALICE (*Sitting*) Yes, of course.

XENIA (*Facing* JUNE) I require a personal possession from you—(JUNE *looks startled*)—to hold in my hand. To connect with your vibrations. Anything—a piece of jewelry—

JUNE I don't wear jewelry. Will a hanky do?

XENIA (*Taking* JUNE's *handkerchief*) Beautiful. Now, to work . . . First, a warning. Next week will be tough for Sagittarians. Mars is in conjunction with Venus. And I don't have to tell you what that means. (*She sits down and shuffles a pack of cards*) Cut the cards.

JUNE (*Cutting the cards*) All right?

XENIA Again. (JUNE *cuts again*) And once more, just for luck—

ALICE —as the bishop said to the actress.

JUNE (*Sternly*) We can dispense with observations from the East.

XENIA (*Scrutinizing the cards*) A short journey to see a friend; a pleasant surprise; unexpected money; the Queen of Spades—a woman in black you do not like?

ALICE The Mother Superior?

JUNE Shut up!

XENIA Whoever it is—keep out of her way—she's no good to you.

JUNE (*Stuttering*) What—what is she going to do?

XENIA (*Consulting the cards*) She's asking you to a big do.

JUNE (*Incredulous*) The Mother Superior?
      (ALICE *giggles*)

XENIA I see lots of people, lots of drink, dancing . . .

ALICE (*Brightly*) I know! It's not the convent—it's the drag ball at Richmond!

XENIA (*She continues laying the cards*) Maybe a slight emotional upset—nothing serious. You hear of a broken romantic association . . . You catch a cold. A very bad cold!

JUNE (*Alarmed*) When?

XENIA (*Thoughtfully*) Maybe it's because I'm holding your handkerchief . . . Forget the cold. What else—?
      (*She looks at the cards again*)

37

JUNE My career . . .

XENIA I can see a red-headed man.

JUNE Ginger the pubkeeper! What's he doing?

XENIA I'm afraid it's not very clear . . . Ah! I see a letter
—a very important letter . . .

ALICE (*Suddenly remembering*) The envelope!

JUNE (*Jumping up, panic-stricken*) The envelope!

ALICE *and* JUNE (*Gasping*) The envelope . . .

XENIA (*Helpfully*) It could be a postcard.

ALICE (*Snatches the hidden letter from behind the cushion. To* JUNE) Here it is! Do you want to open it?

JUNE (*Anguished*) No.

ALICE Let's send it back to her, tell her she must have
dropped it out of her bag.

JUNE No, no. It's fallen into our hands; we'd better read
it.

XENIA May I see the envelope?

JUNE Yes, of course. Do you—do you get any . . . vibrations?

XENIA (*Carefully*) Mmm . . . It's difficult to say. It could
mean one of two things . . .

JUNE (*Squaring her shoulders*) Give it to me! I'm going
to open it. (*She takes the envelope from* MADAME XENIA,
and tears it open) What must be, must be . . . (*She*

38

glances at the contents, and collapses onto the settee)
Oh, my God!

ALICE (*Rushing to comfort her*)   George! What's the matter? George! (JUNE *remains impassive;* MADAME XENIA *has taken the letter and looks at it*) What does it say?

XENIA   "Memo from Audience Research. Latest Popularity Ratings: Sister George 64.5 per cent. Ginger Hopkins 68."

JUNE   That's the weapon they've been waiting for. Now they'll kill me.

Curtain

Beryl Reid as SISTER GEORGE

Act Two

Scene One

A week later. It is 4 A.M. By the dim light of a table lamp JUNE *can be discerned, sitting at the table. She is wearing a dressing gown; in front of her is a tumbler and a bottle of gin. She is roused from her torpor by the ringing of an alarm clock in the bedroom.*

JUNE (*Startled*) What . . . ? It must be morning . . . I must have dropped off . . . (*Calling*) Childie! Rise and shine—that's if you persist in this ridiculous enterprise! Childie? I'm in the living room.

ALICE (*Dressed only in brassière and pants, carrying a bundle of clothing in her arms, comes running in. She throws her clothes on the settee, and attacks* JUNE) Pinch, punch, first of the month!

JUNE (*Jumping up*) Are you out of your mind?

ALICE (*Squashed*) It's the first of the month . . . October . . .

JUNE You could have given me a heart attack.

ALICE Sorry.

JUNE Gawd Almighty . . . What's the time?

ALICE Ten to four.

JUNE When are you supposed to get there?

ALICE There's no rush; the gang gets there at about five. Have you made out your list?

JUNE No.

43

ALICE (*Annoyed*) Well, why didn't you? Are you sure you don't want me to try for *Swan Lake*?

JUNE Positive. I can't stand those bloody little cygnets prancing about—in their tutus—

ALICE All right, all right. Nobody's forcing you.

JUNE (*Rising, stretching out her arms*) My sympathy's entirely with Von Rothbart—

ALICE I'll just try for *Giselle* then.

JUNE Yeah, you try. And *Petrushka*; don't forget *Petrushka*.

ALICE You told me last night you didn't want to see *Petrushka*!

JUNE Did I? Well, I changed my mind . . .

ALICE (*Exasperated, getting hold of the program*) Oh, you are a nuisance! I'd put a tick against *Petrushka* and then I crossed it out, and now I've got to put a tick again . . . and now I can't find it—

JUNE You're annoying me, you know . . . Stop getting so . . . so het-up about your bloody ballet.

ALICE It's all very well for you to talk—you'll be sitting at home. There's a big queue, and if you don't know what to ask for—

JUNE You've got hours to decide what to ask for! You're only queuing for your queue tickets now.

ALICE I know. But we've all got our lists. Anyway, there's no certainty that we get what we ask for: you only get so many for Fonteyn and Nureyev—

JUNE   In that case: why make a list?

ALICE   (*On the brink of hysteria*)   You've got to ask for it first, even if you don't get it!

JUNE   You'll get something you're *not* asking for in a minute.

ALICE   Anyway, it wouldn't have hurt you to have come with me. You're up.

JUNE   I wouldn't be seen dead with that mob. What a collection!

ALICE   There's nothing wrong with them. They're very nice, the regulars, I've known some of them for fifteen years. Do you know: there's a woman there who follows Anya Linden everywhere . . .

JUNE   *Everywhere?*

ALICE   Oh, shut up.

JUNE   Anyway, I did come with you one day—remember? Never again. All that gossip and name-dropping—

ALICE   The only reason you didn't like it was because you were embarrassed by the lorry-driver.

JUNE   What lorry-driver?

ALICE   The one that called at you, "That's a nice pair of head-lamps."

JUNE   I had totally forgotten. Besides, he was paying me a compliment—unlike the gentleman in Soho, who suggested that you should wear a pair of sunglasses for a brassière!

ALICE   Don't be disgusting.

JUNE (*Jeering*)   You're my flatmate in more senses than one.

ALICE (*Incensed*)   George, don't drink any more.

JUNE (*Dangerously*)   Mind your own business.

ALICE   Night after night I find you sitting up—with the bottle of gin and that old press-cuttings book. And then you wonder why you're tired.

JUNE   I can't sleep.

ALICE   You don't try. You must try to relax, to unwind—

JUNE (*Imitating her caustically*)   Relax! Unwind! It's easy for you to talk—

ALICE   You've been impossible ever since that day Mrs. Mercy came to tea—

JUNE   Well, I'm more impossible since I ran into her again yesterday.

ALICE   Where?

JUNE   At BH.

ALICE   Was she friendly?

JUNE   She smiled at me—with the same expression as my old cat Tiddles had when she used to look in a goldfish bowl. Until one Sunday my parents and I came home from church, and there on the table lay the goldfish—all five of them—neatly laid out, like sardines . . .

ALICE   Did she . . . say anything to you?

JUNE I'll show you what she did. Get up. Go on, stand up a minute. (ALICE *stands up*) You're me. I was just coming out from the studio, on my way to the canteen, when I turned a corner rather sharply, and ran slap into her. Go on—bump into me.

ALICE No, I don't want to do that.

JUNE Don't be soppy . . . Go on—bump into me! (ALICE *brushes against* JUNE) Oh, God help us! No, properly, stupid. Hard. Try again.

ALICE I've got to go in a minute.

JUNE You'll bloody well stay till I've done with you. Now then—you're coming down the corridor. (*She claps her hands*) Start!

ALICE (*Takes a run, bumps into* JUNE, *and floors her*) Sorry!

JUNE (*Rises*) "Oh, it's you." (*She surveys her with Mrs. Mercy's half-smile*) "Chin up, Sister George." (*She pats her arm, and walks past her*) Chin up, indeed, the lousy old cow. You noticed the way she patted my arm—as if to say: "Sorry, it can't be helped."

ALICE You're imagining things again.

JUNE She's been avoiding me, I tell you, and I know why . . .

ALICE She was probably in a hurry to get somewhere. A committee meeting or something.

JUNE They've had that. And I found out what happened.

ALICE (*Alarmed*) What?

47

JUNE I've been written out of next Tuesday's episode.

ALICE What?

JUNE Are you deaf? I said—

ALICE I heard. So what—it's happened before. Every time you go on holiday—

JUNE But I'm not going on holiday, am I? (ALICE *is silent*) Sister George is confined to her bed . . . with a bad cold . . .

ALICE That in itself—

JUNE (*Cutting her short*) That in itself could mean it's a dress rehearsal for my extinction.

ALICE Nothing of the sort.

JUNE They want to see what it sounds like without me . . . if I am expendable . . .

ALICE What about the following episodes?

JUNE (*Grimly*) We shall know soon. The new scripts are due in the post this morning. I can see what's going to happen. That cold's going to get worse—I can feel it in my bones. It'll turn into bronchitis, then pneumonia, and before I know where I am I shall be out like a light.

ALICE (*Only half-convinced*) You are making a mountain out of a molehill. You've missed episodes before . . . it's nothing to lose sleep over—

JUNE That's what you think . . . Anyway, I'm not the only one.

ALICE What do you mean?

48

JUNE Did you know that you talk in your sleep?

ALICE I don't.

JUNE You do. I heard you distinctly. Last night and again tonight. You woke me up.

ALICE (*Nervously*) What did I say?

JUNE You were tossing about, and mumbling something. And then out it came, loud and clear.

ALICE (*Unconvinced*) What?

JUNE (*In a plaintive, high-pitched voice*) "Take me!"

ALICE You're lying!

JUNE (*As before*) "Take me, Isadore!"

ALICE That's a filthy lie, and you know it!

JUNE The "Isadore" wasn't any too distinct: it might have been another name.

ALICE I don't believe a word of this.

JUNE (*More in sorrow than in anger*) You're having an affair with someone, aren't you?

ALICE I wish I were.

JUNE (*Crushed*) That was very . . . unkind.

ALICE Well, you asked for it. Always nagging me. Even if I did shout "Take me" in my sleep—and I am not aware of it—

JUNE You couldn't be: you were asleep at the time.

49

ALICE   All right: even if I did, it might have meant "take me for a walk" or (*Brightly*)—"Take me to the ballet!"

JUNE   A likely story!

ALICE   You always put the nastiest interpretation on what people say.

JUNE   In nine cases out of ten it's true. (*Sipping her gin*) Are you making yourself some breakfast?

ALICE   Just a cup of coffee. I usually have a hot pie later on with the gang. In one of the workmen's cafés. It's ever such fun, really! You get the ballet crowd and the night shift from Covent Garden market all mixing together.

JUNE   Sounds scintillating.

ALICE   It's ever so lively. Why don't you get dressed and come? They'd be thrilled to see you, and everyone would ask for your autograph!

JUNE   (*High-pitched*)   "Take me!"

ALICE   Oh, George!

JUNE   No, you run along and enjoy yourself . . . I'm all right where I am . . . waiting for the scripts to arrive.

ALICE   I don't know what's the matter with you just lately! You've become really . . . morbid. You used to be such fun.

JUNE   What are you talking about? We're going to the fancy dress ball tonight, aren't we? I bet it'll be you who'll be tired and wan tonight—after getting up at this unearthly hour!

ALICE   I'm glad you said that. I must take my iron pills.
That'll help to keep me awake!
    (*She takes a bottle from the sideboard, shakes a pill
    out and swallows it*)

JUNE   Let me see them.

ALICE   What for?

JUNE (*Emphatically*)   Let me see them!

ALICE (*Handing her the bottle*)   All right . . .

JUNE (*Examining it*)   Why doesn't it say what they are?
(ALICE *looks nonplussed*) There's no name on the label!

ALICE   I don't know.

JUNE (*Scrutinizing it*)   All it says—(*she has difficulty in
deciphering the writing in the dark*)—is 'One to be
taken every day, as prescribed'. (*She sniffs the bottle*)
I don't believe these are iron pills at all . . . They're those
birth pills—

ALICE   Oh, really? Dr. Kunjaghari gave them to me. Why
don't you go and ask him?

JUNE (*Viciously*)   Because I don't trust Dr. Kunjaghari,
that's why. He's a quack. He's like those Indians who
come to the door in a turban, flogging brass bangles for
rheumatism!

ALICE   Perhaps you'd like to have them chemically ana-
lyzed.

JUNE   It would shake you if I did, wouldn't it?

ALICE   You can do what you like—you'd only make yourself ridiculous. Like that time you rang at the office, pretending to be Mrs. Katz.

JUNE   It served its purpose—it gave him a fright!

ALICE   It very nearly got me the sack. He knew it was you.

JUNE   He couldn't prove it.

ALICE   He's a solicitor—he could prove anything! (*Rummaging among her clothes*) Can't find my socks.

JUNE   I say—(*Regarding her benignly*) Seeing you in black pants reminds me of the army. We all had to wear regulation black woollen pants. We used to refer to them as black-outs. One day, a chap came to talk to us on the subject, "What not to do with our black-outs down." He couldn't understand why we kept giggling . . .

ALICE   (*Putting on her socks*)   Found them!

JUNE   Your legs are unusually white—luminous white. Loo-minous . . . I don't think I've ever seen such white legs.

ALICE   They don't get much sun on them.

JUNE   There's something uniquely touching about white legs . . . especially when they are loo-minous white . . . You're very pale altogether. You're anaemic—you ought to take iron pills. (ALICE *throws her a meaningful glance*) I mean proper pills . . . not that muck.
(*She pours herself another gin*)

ALICE   Haven't you had enough?

JUNE (*Quickly*)   No. (*Chuckling, raising her glass*) To absent friends. Your health, albino mice!

ALICE   You *are* naughty.

JUNE   Say that again.

ALICE   What?

JUNE   What you just said.

ALICE   You *are* naughty?

JUNE   That's it. The same inflection. Takes me back years . . .

ALICE   You mean—

JUNE   When we first met—in Mrs. Goodbody's tastefully furnished bedsitters . . . I used to watch you come and go—for weeks I watched you—and never said a word to you.

ALICE   You were different then—you hadn't become famous.

JUNE   Every morning I used to watch you go to work. Punctually at ten past nine every morning. You were always in a rush.

ALICE   I had to get on the underground at twenty past—

JUNE   Often you were in such a hurry you would fall over the doorstep; or, if it had been raining, you'd come slithering out, shouting "Oops"—

ALICE   I had no idea you were watching me.

JUNE   One night, I went into the bathroom just after you'd had a bath. The mirrors were all steamed up, and the bathmat was moist and glistening where you'd stood on it. There was a smell of talcum powder and of bath

53

crystals—it was like an enchanted wood . . . I stood quite still on that mat—in your footsteps—and I saw that you'd left your comb behind. It was a small pink plastic comb, and it had your hairs in it. I took that comb back to my room and kept it as a souvenir . . . And all this time I'd never spoken a word to you . . .

ALICE   You soon made up for it.

JUNE   That night your boy friend saw you home . . . I knew I'd have to strike quickly.

ALICE   That was Roger. He wanted to marry me.

JUNE (*Bitterly*)   That's what they all said—and you fell for it, silly goose.

ALICE   Some of them meant it; Roger meant it.

JUNE   What are you talking about? Roger was already married!

ALICE (*Adamantly*)   He still meant it. I liked Roger; he had a ginger moustache . . .

JUNE   What a lot of rubbish. His moustache was ginger because he used to singe it with his cigarettes—you told me so yourself. You told me that being kissed by him tasted all sort of burnt and beery.

ALICE   I might have had babies . . .
(*Long pause*)

JUNE (*Quietly*)   You haven't been lonely, exactly.

ALICE (*Changing the subject*)   There's a performance of *Petrushka* on the nineteenth. I might try for that

JUNE (*Suddenly*)   Shh! Shh! Was that the post?

ALICE At this time in the morning? It won't be here for hours yet. You really ought to go to bed . . .
    (*There is a pause*)

JUNE (*Seriously*) They're driving me round the bend.

ALICE You're driving yourself round the bend! Why don't you go to bed?

JUNE Because I can't sleep.

ALICE Shall I get you some hot milk?

JUNE Urghh!

ALICE You'll catch a cold, you know, sitting up like this.

JUNE I've already got a cold.

ALICE Well, keep your throat covered up, then. Put your dressing gown on properly. It's time we got you a new one—this collar is all frayed . . . come on, tuck it in . . . I'll put some new braid on it tomorrow . . . there, better?

JUNE Thanks.

ALICE Shall I put the bottle away?

JUNE No, I just want to hold it for a moment.

ALICE I ought to be going—it's half past four. Will you be all right?

JUNE Childie, they won't do it, will they? They *can't*, after all I've done for them.

ALICE Of course they can't, George. You must stop brooding about it, you'll make yourself ill. Why don't you go to bed and sleep it off? You can set the alarm to wake you for rehearsal.

JUNE   There's no rehearsal tomorrow.

ALICE   All right, then. Good. You can get a nice long rest. Now, George, I've got to go.

JUNE   No, wait a minute—

ALICE   Oh, George, they'll be waiting for me, I'll be at the back of the queue.

JUNE   You can't go like *that*, you know.

ALICE   Like what?

JUNE   (*Pointing to the knapsack*)   You're not going on a hike, you know. Mind you: donkeys are best for loading.

ALICE   There's only a change of clothing in it, to take to the office. And a few provisions. Please, may I go now?

JUNE   Did you speak?

ALICE   Yes, I said, "May I go now?"

JUNE   (*Considering the request*)   Not before you have made your obeisance to me in the proper manner.

ALICE   (*Alarmed*)   What do you mean?

JUNE   (*Breathing heavily and alcoholically for a few moments*)   Kiss the hem of my garment. (*With an imperious gesture*)   On your knees. Go on! Down, boy, down!
(*She snaps her fingers*)

ALICE   (*Picks up her knapsack, looks at her watch, and shrugs her shoulders*)   Oh, all right.
(*She goes on her knees*)

JUNE   Now repeat after me: I hereby solemnly swear—

ALICE   (*Mechanically*)   I hereby solemnly swear—

JUNE   That I will not allow—

ALICE   That I will not allow—

JUNE   Anybody whosoever, including Mr. Katz, gratification of his fleshly instincts with me today or at any other time.

ALICE   (*Quickly*)   All right, all right, I swear.

JUNE   Mind you remember, or may the curse of Satan fall on your head!

ALICE   (*Quickly reiterating*)   That's one *Giselle*, one *Petrushka*, and no *Lac*—

JUNE   (*With enormous effort*)   *Rien de Lac de Cygnes. C'est juste* (*Holds on to* ALICE's scarf) *Mon petit chou.*

ALICE   George, let go. Let go!

JUNE   What's this?

ALICE   What?

JUNE   (*Looking at the label on scarf*)   This isn't yours, is it? Where did you get it?

ALICE   George, give it back.

JUNE   Who is J. V. S. Partridge?

ALICE   A young Liberal. Satisfied?

JUNE   Far, far from satisfied. How long have you been entangled with this—youth?

ALICE He's not a youth. He's forty-six.

JUNE Bit long in the tooth for a young Liberal? (*Fiercely*) Who is he?

ALICE The chap downstairs, daftie. Madame Xenia's lodger.

JUNE Ah—I thought there was some monkey business going on.

ALICE There is not. I've only ever seen him twice.

JUNE How did you get his scarf, then?

ALICE I pinched it off the hall-stand.

JUNE D'you expect me to believe that?

ALICE Look, George. I've never even spoken to him. It's nothing.

JUNE That's what you said when you went off with that estate agent for a week-end in Birmingham.

ALICE That was five years ago—

JUNE It happened once—it can happen again—

ALICE (*Almost screaming*) Nothing happened!

JUNE What?

ALICE *Nothing!*

JUNE Well, nothing's going to happen with this one. I forbid you to speak to him again.

ALICE You're raving mad. He's a neighbor, there's no harm in being friendly.

JUNE (*Shouting*) I forbid you to speak to him, do you hear?

ALICE (*Shouting back*) I'll flipping well speak to him if I want to—why shouldn't I?

JUNE (*Venomously*) You fancy him, don't you?

ALICE He seems perfectly agreeable—(*Sees* JUNE'S *face contorted with suspicion*) Yes, I do fancy him—he's a dish. (JUNE *threatens her*) You keep away from me— you've no right to—

JUNE I've got every right.

ALICE I'm not married to you, you know. (*Long pause*) I'm sorry, George, but you asked for it.

JUNE You'd better run along, you'll be late.

ALICE Look after yourself! Don't forget the party tonight! (*Exits*)

JUNE (*Alone, wanders about the room. Surveys the scene for a few moments, swaying slightly. Then pulling a chair center stage*) Ah, there's my beautiful bike. Mornin', old friend! Just get you started in a minute. (*She sits astride it, and makes a purring noise to indicate the start of the engine*) Prrrrrrrrrrrrrrrr—prr— prrr—(*She waves*) 'Bye Jean, 'Bye Rosie, tell your dad to look after his gammy leg! Prrrr—prrrr—(*She starts singing*) "Oh God, our help in ages past"—prr—prr —"Our hope for years to come,"—Prrr—prrr—Morning, Ginger, morning, Vicar, you're up early today—prrr— prrr—first call old Mrs. Hinch—prrrr—prrrr—"Be thou our guard while troubles last"—prrr—prr—"And our eternal"—prrr—"home."

Scene Two

Later, the same day.
The stage is empty when the curtain rises. Laughter and
shrieks can be heard from off stage.

JUNE (*Imperiously, off stage*)   Pull yourself together. Try
again, and this time do it properly!

ALICE (*Off stage*)   I can't promise I'll get it right.
(*The well-known signature tune of Laurel and*
Hardy is heard, laboriously played on the flute.
ALICE *and* JUNE *enter, in the costume of Laurel and*
Hardy)

JUNE (*Imitating* HARDY)   And what, may I ask, are you
supposed to be doing?

ALICE   Nothing, Olly, just playing . . . a tune . . .

JUNE   May I suggest that you stop playing a tune . . . and
get on with the next bit. A-one, a-two.

JUNE and ALICE (*Doing a soft-shoe dance, side by side*)
"By the light—dum da dum da dum—of the silvery
moon—dum da dum—I used to—rum dum da dum da
dum da dum—with my honey and—La da da. By the
light—"
(ALICE *bumps into* JUNE)

JUNE   What was the meaning of that?
(*Hits* ALICE *with her bowler hat*)

ALICE   Nothing, Olly—I was only—practicing—

60

JUNE (*Turning away in dismay, fluttering her tie*) Oh, fiddlesticks . . .

ALICE Did you say "fiddlesticks"?
(*She rams the flute into* JUNE)

JUNE (*Forgetting her impersonation*) Ouch, that hurt! That was not funny!

ALICE (*Giggling*) Sorry, Olly.

JUNE (*Giving* ALICE *a great swipe*) Sorry, Stan.

ALICE (*As herself*) That hurt!

JUNE (*In the best Hardy manner, dusting her hands*) Let that be a lesson to you!
(*She turns away, beaming*)

ALICE (*Again rams the flute against* JUNE. JUNE *seizes it viciously*) Be careful, it's Miss Broadbent's—

JUNE (*Only half acting*) A very useful instrument.
(*She hits* ALICE *over the head with it—fortunately she has her bowler on*)

ALICE (*Squaring up to* JUNE, *making sounds of frustrated rage*) You, oh . . .

JUNE (*Under her breath*) That's not Laurel, daftie, that's the Three Stooges!

ALICE Sorry, Olly. (*Brightly*) Olly—

JUNE Yep?

ALICE Give me your hat.

JUNE What for, Stan?

ALICE I just want to look at something.

JUNE (*Thrusting her hat at* ALICE) O.K. (ALICE *spits on it, and puts it on* JUNE's *head again.* JUNE, *as herself*) What was that supposed to be?

ALICE (*As herself*) Don't know. Just an idea. Horseplay, you know . . . We're celebrating because you're back in the series, aren't we?

JUNE (*With an evil glint in her eye*) Just because the scriptwriters have cured my cold . . . there's no need to go raving, bloody mad you know.

ALICE I thought it was funny.

JUNE You thought it was funny?

ALICE Yes, I thought it was funny.

JUNE You thought it was funny. Stan.

ALICE Yes, Olly?

JUNE Give me your hat.

ALICE What for?

JUNE I just want to look at something. Look up there, Stan.

ALICE There's nothing up there, Olly.

JUNE Try this, then, Stan.
(ALICE *hands over her bowler:* JUNE *with a right-eous nod of the head goes to the table and squirts soda into* ALICE's *hat.* ALICE *stands, unconcernedly twiddling her thumbs.* JUNE *returns, and places the hat, brimful with soda water, on* ALICE)

ALICE   You fool—now you've spoilt my costume!
(*She attacks* JUNE, *pummelling her with her fists*)

JUNE (*Keeping her at arm's length*)   Steady, now. Steady.

ALICE   What was the point of that?

JUNE   Just an idea. Horseplay, you know.

ALICE   You are rotten. I'm all wet, Now I'll have to change.

JUNE   Nonsense, woman. A drop of good clear water never did anybody any harm.

ALICE   All right.
(*She takes some flowers out of a vase, and approaches* JUNE, *menacingly holding the vase*)

JUNE   Don't come near me! I warn you: keep away.

ALICE   I want to show you something, Olly.

JUNE   Childie, stop it. Be your age.
(*She backs away*)

ALICE   Take your punishment like a man!

JUNE (*Shouting*)   All right. (*She stands stock-still, squaring her shoulders*) Go on—what are you waiting for?
(*They laugh, and struggle with the vase*)

ALICE (*Losing her nerve*)   Never mind.
(*She puts the vase on the table*)

JUNE   Go on—I'm not afraid of a drop of water! Ugh, you're like a marshmallow.
(*The doorbell rings*)

63

ALICE   It's Madame Xenia, to fetch us. She's ordered a cab. She's early.

JUNE   Well, don't stand and gape. Open the door!
(She propels ALICE *to the door with a kick)*

ALICE   *(Off-stage)*   Oh! Oh, I'm sorry . . . We were expecting—
(She ushers in MRS. MERCY CROFT*)*

MRS. MERCY   I'm sorry to intrude. I do hope it's not inconvenient . . .

JUNE   *(Taken aback)*   Not at all. I'm sorry we're . . .

MRS. MERCY   Playing charades?

ALICE   As a matter of fact, we were just getting ready to go out—to a fancy dress ball.

JUNE   Ball—fancy—

MRS. MERCY   Oh, I'll come back another time when it's more convenient. Perhaps Miss Buckridge could come to see me tomorrow morning, before rehearsal?

JUNE   We're not in a rush. We can talk now. Would you have a drink?

MRS. MERCY   No thank you.

ALICE   *(Cordially)*   Do sit down, Mrs. Mercy.

MRS. MERCY   Thank you, dear.

JUNE   If you had telephoned a little earlier—

MRS. MERCY   *I know*. It's most remiss of me, turning up unexpectedly like this. Actually, I've come straight from a meeting—felt I had to see you personally.

ALICE (*Anxiously*)   The nuns?

MRS. MERCY   Oh, didn't the office tell you? We had a most charming communication from the Mother Superior. All is forgiven. But there's still the matter of the charity.

JUNE   What charity?

ALICE   The donation you promised to give to the convent.

JUNE   Oh, that!

MRS. MERCY   It's only obliquely mentioned in the letter—

JUNE (*With a wry smile*)   I didn't expect her to forget about it. (*To* ALICE) Remind me to send her a check tomorrow. It'll keep her Irish novices in hair shirts!

MRS. MERCY   Very nice of you, Miss Buckridge. I'm relieved to see the matter settled.

JUNE (*Going to the cigarette box*)   May I offer you a small cigar?

MRS. MERCY   Oh, no . . . no, thank you. I gave up smoking years ago.

JUNE   You don't mind if I smoke?

MRS. MERCY   Well . . .

ALICE (*Chiding*)   You smoke far too much!

JUNE (*With a mock bow*)   Thank you for your touching concern.

MRS. MERCY   Well now, I'm afraid I have some bad news for you, Miss Buckridge.

JUNE Bad news . . . ?

MRS. MERCY You're the first to be told. It's only just been decided; or rather, it's only just received the official stamp of approval . . .

ALICE (*Terrified*) You can't mean—

JUNE Be quiet, Childie.

MRS. MERCY Yes. I'm sorry, Miss Buckridge: it's the end of Sister George.
    (*There is a stunned pause*)

ALICE (*Suddenly shouting*) But why? Why?

MRS. MERCY Believe me, dear Miss Buckridge, the decision is no reflection on your ability as an actress. You created a character that has become a nation-wide favorite.

ALICE (*Still incredulous*) But why kill her?

MRS. MERCY Why do some of our nearest and dearest have to die? Because that's life. In Applehurst we try to re-create the flavor of life, as it is lived in hundreds of English villages—

ALICE But she's the most popular character in it!

MRS. MERCY (*Slightly uncomfortable*) I know. The BBC took that into consideration. They felt—and I must say I concurred—that only some dramatic event, something that would get into the news headlines, could save Applehurst. We felt that in their grief, robbed of one of their greatest favorites, listeners would return again to Applehurst with a new loyalty, with a—

JUNE (*Interrupting dully*) How?

MRS. MERCY (*Quietly*) It's not for another fortnight. It's scheduled for the twelfth.

JUNE But how?

MRS. MERCY (*Smiling benignly*) It's just an ordinary morning at Applehurst. The chaffinch on Sister George's window wakes her up as usual and is rewarded with its daily saucerful of crumbs—

JUNE (*Under her breath, automatically*) Hello, Dicky . . .

MRS. MERCY Up in the road, in the Old Mill Farm, young Jimmy Bromley, the scamp, wakes up with a cough and doesn't want to go to school. "We'd better get Sister George in," says his mother—and he's up in a jiffy! Meanwhile, punctual to the minute, Sister George finishes her breakfast and packs a basketful of preserves and cottage cheese for old Mrs. Hinch, in bed with bronchitis. On with her bonnet and cape, and off she goes, striding purposefully through the autumn leaves— sound effects here—to the bicycle shed. The bolts are pushed back, and the door creaks open, and there's her prized possession—the motorbike.

JUNE Good morning, old friend.

MRS. MERCY Whiz—pop—the engine starts—and away she goes! Pop-pop-pop-pop . . . "Hurry up, Jimmy, you'll be late for school . . ." she calls out. "Tell Mrs. Pemberton to give you plenty of homework to keep you out of mischief!" "I will," the boy calls back—adding, as she drives out of earshot—"I don't think!"

JUNE Cheeky little beggar!

67

MRS. MERCY   A chorus of greetings follow her as she heads out into the open country—the wind billowing in her cape—and bursts, as usual, into a snatch of her favorite hymn: "O God, Our Help in Ages Past." Honk-honk answers her hooter in a merry descant as she turns into Oakmead Road, and then—BANG! (*She claps her hands*) Collision with a ten-ton truck.

JUNE   Oh, my God . . .

ALICE   Is it—is it . . .

MRS. MERCY   Instantaneous. Never regains consciousness.

ALICE (*Has started to cry*)   You can't, you can't . . .

MRS. MERCY   It so happens that your death will coincide with Road Safety Week: a cause which we know has been close to you for many years.

JUNE (*Recovering slightly*)   I've never ridden carelessly. (*Rising*) I protest—

MRS. MERCY (*Anxious to placate her*)   I know, I know. We're taking great care to establish it's the lorry driver's fault.

JUNE (*Unconvinced*)   But even so—a ten-ton truck . . .

MRS. MERCY   I'm sorry, but there it is.

JUNE (*With dignity*)   I think I have a right to a say about my own mode of death!

MRS. MERCY (*Kindly*)   Now, do leave it to us, dear Miss Buckridge. Leave it to the BBC. We know best. We've had experience in these matters.

68

JUNE   If I could die in the course of duty—from some infection, perhaps—an epidemic. Yes, that's it—I could go to nurse a patient somewhere up in the hills, someone suffering from some unspeakable disease . . .

MRS. MERCY   I'm sorry, Miss Buckridge, the scripts have been typed.

JUNE   But they could be altered . . .

MRS. MERCY   I'm afraid they've been officially approved.

JUNE   Then I shall take this to a higher authority—

ALICE   Yes, don't let them treat you like this. You've still got your public behind you: they won't let them kill you off!

MRS. MERCY   (Annoyed)   I'm surprised at your attitude, Miss McNaught: I thought you'd be more sensible. I've come here of my own volition, as a gesture of courtesy to a valued and trusted colleague.

ALICE   But it's not fair!

JUNE   Shut up, Childie.

ALICE   I won't shut up.

MRS. MERCY   I was going to say that I'm sure the BBC will want to find some outlet for Miss Buckridge's talents.

JUNE   I'm still not satisfied about the—the accident.

MRS. MERCY   I'm afraid that decision is final.

ALICE   (To JUNE)   Do you think you ought to lie down? You look awful. (To MRS. MERCY) She hasn't been sleeping well lately.

69

MRS. MERCY   Oh, I'm sorry to hear that.

JUNE (*Pause*)   Will I be buried in the churchyard?

MRS. MERCY (*Cheerfully*)   It'll be done in style! Don't you worry your head about that. There's some talk of a special memorial broadcast, with contributions from all sorts of famous people—but I shouldn't really be talking about that, as it's still in the planning stage.

JUNE   Would I be in it? In the memorial broadcast, I mean?

MRS. MERCY   Naturally. There will be lots of recorded extracts of Sister George.

JUNE   No, I meant: would I be able to tell the people how the character developed?

MRS. MERCY   Oh no! That would spoil the illusion.

JUNE   But you said just now you wanted to use me again.

MRS. MERCY   Yes, but not as Sister George.

JUNE (*On the brink of hysteria*)   What's wrong with Sister George?

MRS. MERCY   Nothing, dear Miss Buckridge. She'd be dead, that's all.
(*Pause*)

ALICE (*To* JUNE)   Come on, George, come and lie down. Come on—come on.

MRS. MERCY   In due course, I hope to discuss ideas for a new serial with you. We'll do something really exciting; I'm sure of it!

JUNE   Mrs. Mercy: I would like to thank you for coming personally to tell me of the . . . decision. I don't really feel up to discussing new ideas for serials at the moment.

MRS. MERCY   Of course you don't!

JUNE   Please don't go. Childie—Miss McNaught—will make you a cup of tea or something. I'll go and lie down for a bit, I think. I'll put that away, in the . . . cabinet. (*Taking gin bottle*).

ALICE   Will you be all right, George?

JUNE (*Stopping in the doorway*)   What did you say?

ALICE   I said: Will you be all right?

JUNE   You called me "George" then, didn't you? You'll have to get out of that habit.
(*She exits*)

MRS. MERCY (*Rising*)   I really don't think I should stay any longer.

ALICE   Please stay, Mrs. Mercy. I'd like you to.

MRS. MERCY   Well, of course . . . if I can be of any assistance—

ALICE (*With an awkward laugh*)   Just to have somebody to talk to . . .

MRS. MERCY   I expect it hasn't been easy for you . . . recently.

ALICE (*Quietly, with an anxious look to the door*)   She's been impossible. Life's been absolute hell. You've no idea.

MRS. MERCY   I thought as much.

ALICE   Night after night I found her sitting up, drinking. Said she couldn't sleep with worry—

MRS. MERCY   Did she keep you awake?

ALICE   Some nights she made such a din—singing and, you know, reciting and things—that the neighbors complained!

MRS. MERCY   I had no idea it was as bad as that!

ALICE   It's been . . . diabolical!

MRS. MERCY   I do feel sorry for you.

ALICE   When she gets excited, or nervous, or anything, she has to take it out on somebody. Who do you think bears the brunt? Yours truly.

MRS. MERCY   I'm amazed you put up with it.

ALICE   I have no alternative.

MRS. MERCY   Oh come, there must be lots of openings for a girl with your qualifications!

ALICE   I've been with George for seven years.

MRS. MERCY   Seven years—as long as that!

ALICE   Yes, she was quite unknown when we first met.

MRS. MERCY   I expect she was easier to get on with in those days.

ALICE   She was always very jealous; wouldn't let anyone come near me.

MRS. MERCY   What a shame. Especially as it's so important

for someone with literary ability to have contact with a lot of people.

ALICE How did you know that I—

MRS. MERCY You mentioned your interest in poetry last time we met. You attend classes, I believe?

ALICE Yes, every Wednesday.

MRS. MERCY I'd like to read your poems, if I may?

ALICE Would you? Would you really? Shall I get them now?

MRS. MERCY No, we'd better not disturb Miss Buckridge now! Give me a ring at the BBC and my secretary will fix an appointment.

ALICE Oh, thank you. It's really nice of you . . . to take an interest.

MRS. MERCY Have you ever thought of writing for the radio?

ALICE It has occurred to me. You know: sometimes one hears such tripe, and one thinks—
    (*She puts her hand over her mouth*)

MRS. MERCY (*With mock reproval*) I know what you were going to say!

ALICE Sorry.

MRS. MERCY Never mind. We all feel the same way at times. Anyway, I'm not responsible for *all* the programs!

ALICE I'm sure yours are by far the best.

73

MRS. MERCY (*Very pleased*)   Flattery—

ALICE   No, honestly. Years ago, before I knew you had anything to do with Applehurst, I listened to your talks on the wireless about people's problems and honestly, they were really . . . understanding.

MRS. MERCY (*Touched*)   I'm so glad. (*Indicating the door*) You've got a little problem on *your* hands and no mistake!

ALICE   A big problem!

MRS. MERCY   What are we going to do?

ALICE   Don't know.

MRS. MERCY (*Quietly sympathetic*)   Is she always so difficult?

ALICE   Difficult! She gets very violent—especially after she's had a few pints! You've no idea the things she gets up to!

MRS. MERCY   Really?

ALICE   Oh yes . . . (*See looks round a little wildly*) Mrs. Mercy, I'm scared. I'm scared of what will happen.

MRS. MERCY   Now don't be silly. Nothing will happen. You've been living through a rather difficult few weeks, that's all. It was the uncertainty that made her nervous. Now that she knows the worst she'll be much more bearable, you'll see.

ALICE   You don't know George! I don't know how I'll survive the next fortnight . . .

MRS. MERCY   I'll do what I can to help.

ALICE   I hope she won't get in a rage and murder me.

MRS. MERCY (*Startled*)   Are you serious?

ALICE   Dead serious. When she gets into a temper, she's capable of anything!

MRS. MERCY   Has she ever . . . attacked you?

ALICE   It happens all the time.

MRS. MERCY   But this is *outrageous!*

ALICE   She beats me, you know. She hits me with anything that comes into her hand.

MRS. MERCY (*Horrified*)   But why do you put up with it?

ALICE (*After a pause*)   I have nowhere else to go . . .

MRS. MERCY   Surely there's somewhere . . .

ALICE   I couldn't face living alone. Not any more.

MRS. MERCY (*Overcome*)   My poor girl. This is terrible . . . Look, if there's any more trouble, don't hesitate to give me a ring. Please regard me as your friend.

ALICE   Oh, you really are kind, Mrs. Mercy.

MRS. MERCY   And we must find somewhere for you to go.

ALICE (*Gratefully*)   Would you? Would you really?

MRS. MERCY (*Squeezing* ALICE's *arm*)   Leave it to me. (*Rising*) How pretty this room looks in the evening sun-

75

light . . . All these charming dolls—
(*She picks up Emmeline*)

ALICE That's my favorite. Her name is Emmeline.

MRS. MERCY (*Shaking the doll by the hand*) Hello Emmeline.
(*Pause*)

ALICE Do you think I ought to go and see if George is all right?

MRS. MERCY (*Speaking in a childish voice to the doll*) I should leave her where she is . . . the naughty woman . . .

ALICE I haven't offered you a cup of tea!

MRS. MERCY We haven't time for a cup of tea. We have to go. (*To the doll*) Good-bye, little Emmeline.

ALICE I wish you could stay.

MRS. MERCY So do I. But I'm glad we had a chance to have a little chat. Now remember what I told you; if there's any trouble, get straight on the telephone to me! (ALICE *puts on the bowler hat*) That's the spirit!

ALICE (*In a Laurel voice*) Gee, I'm frightened . . .

MRS. MERCY (*Confidentially*) Don't let her bully you.

ALICE (*As before*) She's a devil when roused . . .

MRS. MERCY Good-bye, dear. Must run. (*Waving from the door*) Have fun.
(*Exits*)

ALICE (*Mechanically*) Must run . . . have fun . . . (*She looks towards the bedroom, undecided; picks up the flute and marches up to the bedroom, playing the Laurel and Hardy signature tune. No reply from* JUNE) George? George, are you all right? (*Still no reply. She hammers on the bedroom door*) George! George!! (*Returning to the room pale with worry*) What am I going to do?

Curtain

Act Three

Heard in darkness before the curtain goes up is the sound of SISTER GEORGE's *motorbike, background of country noises, twittering of birds, mooing, neighing.*

SISTER GEORGE (*Singing*) "Oh God, our help in ages past . . ."
(*Fade out. Then the monotonous sound of the engine of a heavy lorry*)

BILL (*In a thick West Country accent*) You awake, Fred?

FRED (*Grunts something unintelligible*)

BILL Won't do to fall asleep now. We're nearly there.

FRED Not up to it any more . . . this all-night driving.

BILL There's the turning coming up now—don't miss it!

FRED (*Sound of acceleration, and changing of gears*) Let's get there fast—I'm hungry . . .

BILL (*Shouting*) Look out!
(*Screeching of brakes, shouting, followed by an explosion*)

BILL (*Near hysteria*) Fred! We hit her! Fred! We hit her!
(*The sound of a car door slamming is heard*)

FRED It weren't my fault. I braked—

BILL Is she—? My God, she looks bad.

FRED A nurse, by the look of her . . .

BILL (*Calling*) Hey, there!
(*Sound of heavy footsteps, coming nearer*)

FARMER BROMLEY (*Coming nearer*)   What happened?

BILL   Bike came round the corner, fast!

FRED   I tried to brake. It weren't my fault!

FARMER BROMLEY (*Panting*)   I always did say it's a dangerous crossing. Is she badly—Holy Saints! ! It's, it's Sister George!

FRED   It *were*. . . .
> (*The Applehurst theme swells up. The curtain rises*)

Two weeks have passed. It is a sunny October morning. The room is littered with letters and telegrams, and there is an abundance of flowers. MADAME XENIA, *discreetly dressed, is listening to Sister George's accident on a tape recorder. As the Applehurst theme swells up, she switches it off and wipes her eyes.*

XENIA (*Overcome*)   Oi oi oi . . . poor George! (*The doorbell rings*) All right, I come! (*She goes to the front door and opens it*) . . . Yes, I will take them, but I don't know where I am going to put them . . . (*Closes door and comes in with wreaths*) Soon we shall not be able to move. (*Telephone*) They are mad. I told them we were not accepting any more calls. (*She lifts the receiver*) You are mad. I told you we are not accepting any more calls. A message from whom? The girls of your Exchange? Yes, I will convey it . . . Very nice of you . . . Charming. Miss Buckridge will be very touched. Who am I? Never you mind—I am her temporary secretary . . . No, I have nothing to do with Applehurst . . . No, I am not the old gypsy woman who stole a pig! You are beginning to make me very upset. I will not speak any more! And no more calls, if you please! (*She hangs up*) Stupid nit.

(ALICE *enters, rubbing her eyes and yawning. She is wearing baby-doll pajamas*)

ALICE   What time is it?

XENIA *(With a black look)*   Half past ten.

ALICE   Heavens—I'm going to be late for the funeral. (*Nearly trips over a wreath*) Oh, not more flowers—I shall never find my things. . . .

XENIA *(Pointedly)* I have been working for two hours.

ALICE *(Hunting for clothes)*   Where's George?

XENIA   Out.—Gone. I don't know where. I am very worried.

ALICE   Gone? When?

XENIA   Since early this morning. I came up with two wreaths and some lilies—she took one look, rushed into the lift, slammed the gate in my face and went down like a captain on a sinking ship—but not saluting—swearing.

ALICE   I hope she is not going to do something awful?

XENIA   I think she could not stand to be in the flat another moment with all this . . . (*She looks around at the flowers*) She felt claustrophobia—I must get out! It has been terrible for her since the accident—nothing but the telephone—letters—reporters.

ALICE   She ought never to have listened to the accident—it was dreadful.

XENIA   Oi oi oi, I just listened to the tape again—that

beautiful hymn—the screeching brakes, then (*Claps her hands*) crash, bang, wallop!

ALICE (*Covering her ears*) Don't!

XENIA It was like a gas-works blowing up—horrible. (*Shudders*) I cried again.

ALICE Ought we to ring up the police or something?

XENIA No. We must wait. And work. Everything must be right for her when she comes back.
(*She bustles about.* ALICE *sinks into a chair*)

ALICE I feel so exhausted—I think it's the strain.

XENIA Nonsense—it was the farewell party last night. You have no stamina. You are a—what you call it?—a milksop.

ALICE I've probably caught a cold. George stuffed a peach melba down the back of my dress. Really, she's getting worse and worse . . .

XENIA Listen to this. (*Reading the inscription*) "Unforgotten, from the patients and staff of the Sister George Geriatrics Ward." Beautiful! I could cry!

ALICE She'd like that.

XENIA All wreaths against the wall. There. All beautifully organized.

ALICE Honestly, Madame Xenia, you're a brick.

XENIA Why do you say that?

ALICE It's an expression; a friend, a help—

XENIA   I see. But I promised George I would take charge today, and I hold my promise.

ALICE   Could I look at some of the telegrams?

XENIA   If you're very careful and don't get them mixed up. One pile is personal, the other official. Over here it's doubtfuls.

ALICE   Let's see the doubtfuls.

XENIA   What I would like more than anything is a nice cup of tea . . .

ALICE   (*Looking up from a telegram*)   Oh, no!

XENIA   What?

ALICE   (*Bitterly*)   Trust her to get in on the act.
(*She crumples up the telegram*)

XENIA   (*Chiding*)   You must not do this.

ALICE   (*Very red in the face*)   How dare she send telegrams after all these years!

XENIA   From what person . . . ?

ALICE   (*Reading*)   "Heartfelt condolences. Love, Liz."

XENIA   Liz?

ALICE   A friend of George's. Before my time.

XENIA   Aha.

ALICE   An absolute cow. Kept writing sarcastic little notes at first; things like "Hope you are divinely happy" and "Hope this finds you as it leaves me—guess how?"

85

XENIA (*Quietly*) What I would like more than anything is a nice cup of tea . . .

ALICE Anyway, she stole a fountain pen and a camera off George!

XENIA Tut-tut.

ALICE "Heartfelt condolences"—she's mocking her!

XENIA (*Changing the subject*) Here is a nice one from my old friend the Baroness. "Shall be thinking of you to-day. Best wishes for a triumphant funeral. Love, Augusta." She specially put off her hairdresser so that she can listen to it this morning. And she only met George once—at my Hallowe'en party last year.

ALICE Which one was the Baroness?

XENIA She came as Julius Caesar. At least, that's what we *thought* she was meant to be . . .

ALICE I hope George isn't going to be late. . . .

XENIA I think it is a mistake for her to listen today. Psychologically it is a mistake.

ALICE Oh, I don't know. She can't just play a character for six years, and miss her own exit.

XENIA But it will upset her!

ALICE All her old friends will be there—people she's worked with for years. There'll be tributes paid; there'll be a proper service! I mean to say: there's a right way and a wrong way of doing things.
(*She sits on the settee*)

XENIA (*Shrugging her shoulders*) I do not understand you.

ALICE Maybe in your country, people—

XENIA (*Flaring up*) What do you mean: in my country? We had state funerals which could have taught you something: twenty-eight horses with black plumes, ha?

ALICE (*Bitchily*) Well, you had lots of practice, didn't you? All those assassinations—

XENIA Assassinations?

ALICE Shooting people.

XENIA Of course we shoot people we don't like! You send them to the House of Lords—what's the difference?

ALICE Anyway, if you expect the BBC to lay on twenty-eight horses with black plumes, you're in for a disappointment!

XENIA (*Furious*) Do you want me to go? Immediately I go downstairs—

ALICE No, no—

XENIA You can explain my absence to George when she comes back. *If* she comes back . . .
(*She moves to the door*, ALICE *runs after her*)

ALICE No! Madame Xenia, please stay—I didn't mean to be rude. It's my nerves, I'm so worried about her—supposing she's really cracked up and thrown herself under a bus or something—what am I going to do?

XENIA (*After a pause*) No, it is not a bus. (*Mysteriously*)

I read the cards this morning . . . it is something to do with the head.

ALICES   The *head!* Oh, no, . . . I can't bear it.

XENIA (*Suddenly*)   Shh! There's somebody at the door—

ALICE   George!

XENIA   Look cheerful—she must see happy faces.

ALICE   She'll kill me if she sees me walking about like this—
> (ALICE *rushes towards the bedroom, but trips over a large wreath on the way*)

JUNE (*Shouting off*)   Open the windows and let the sunshine in!

XENIA (*Apprehensively*)   We are here, my darling . . .
> (ALICE *picks up the wreath and tries to hide behind it, as* JUNE *sails in, wearing an extravagant pink chiffon hat and carrying a large parcel*)

JUNE   It's glorious out! (*to* XENIA) Darling—how sweet of you to hold the fort—I do hope you weren't pestered too much . . .(ALICE'S *wreath rustles.* JUNE *sees her*) Oh God, down in the forest something stirred.

XENIA   George, we were so worried—where have you been?

JUNE   Shopping. I picked up this marvelous bargain—a Christmas Gift Hamper packed full of goodies (*Unpacking it*) Oh, two bottles of Veuve Clicquot '52.

XENIA   But—what for . . . ?

JUNE   I've decided to skip the funeral and have a celebration.

XENIA   Celebration?

JUNE   Yes, more a coming-out party, really.

XENIA   But who is coming out?

JUNE   I am!

XENIA (*Looking at* JUNE's *hat*)   I see you bought something else, as well . . .

JUNE   Do you like it?

XENIA   It is *charming*! Where did you find it?

JUNE   That little shop on the corner. Saw it in the window and couldn't resist it.

XENIA   You were absolutely right! It does something for you.

JUNE   Do you think so?

XENIA   It makes you look so young! Like eighteen years— (ALICE *sniggers*)

JUNE (*Turning on* ALICE)   What are you laughing at? And why aren't you dressed yet? You look indecent.

ALICE   I overslept. Bit of a hangover.

JUNE (*Incredulous*)   A hangover? After two glasses of shandy?

ALICE   I mixed it a bit.

JUNE   With what—ginger ale? (ALICE *does not reply*) Do

89

you think it proper to entertain visitors in this—this unseemly attire?

XENIA (*Placating*) Oh, please, please.

JUNE Did you make Madame Xenia a cup of tea?

XENIA It really wasn't necessary . . .

JUNE What's the matter with you?

ALICE Don't know.

JUNE You should have been out and about for the last three hours. Did you do your exercises?

ALICE (*Defiantly*) No.

JUNE (*To* MADAME XENIA) Oh God, help us—she takes a keep-fit course. You know: knee bends, running on the spot, bicycling on her back. To judge by her condition it's been singularly ineffective! Go on—I want a cup of tea *now*. And one for Madame Xenia. And get dressed. And look sharpish about it. *Avanti!*

ALICE (*Looking straight at* JUNE) I think your hat is a mistake.

JUNE (*Thundering*) What? (*No reply from* ALICE) I can see this day will end in tears.

ALICE (*Shouting*) They won't be my tears!
(*She runs off*)

JUNE The baggage. The little baggage.

XENIA She is upset.

JUNE She has no business to be upset: it's *my* funeral!

XENIA She's taking it hard. Some people—

JUNE She's no good in a crisis. I've seen it happen again and again: people going to pieces in a crisis. During the war—

XENIA Ah, the war! I was an air raid warden.

JUNE I was in the army. Attached to the Commandos. It was tough, but rewarding.

XENIA It's lucky for her she wasn't old enough.

JUNE Childie in the army? That'd be a bit of a giggle . . . She'd have collapsed under the weight of her forage cap.
    (*She laughs*)

XENIA Would you like to go through the last tributes?

JUNE If it's absolutely necessary.

XENIA Look at this—from the patients and staff of the Sister George Geriatric Ward. In that hospital your name will never die.

JUNE (*Firmly*) *Her* name.

XENIA Her name, your name. It's the same thing—

JUNE Not any longer. George and I have parted company. And do you know, I'm glad to be free of the silly bitch. (*Pause*) Honestly.

XENIA George, what are you saying?

JUNE I'm saying that my name is *June*. June Buckridge. I'm endeavoring to memorize it.

XENIA You are incredible!

JUNE Why?

ALICE (*Entering with the tea tray*) I'm afraid one of the telegrams got crumpled up. You'd better read it.

JUNE What telegram?

ALICE Here. (*She serves the crumpled telegram on a bread plate*) Will there be any reply, Madam?

JUNE (*Reads it*) Liz . . . I don't believe it!

ALICE (*Bitterly*) I thought you'd be pleased.

XENIA (*Attempting to mediate*) It's always nice to hear from old friends.

ALICE (*Starts to sing "Auld Lang Syne"*) Sugar, Madame Xenia?

XENIA No, thank you. I take it neat.

JUNE (*Reminiscing*) She was a real thoroughbred: stringy, nervy, temperamental. I remember I used to tease her because her hair grew down her neck, like a thin mane, between her shoulder blades— (ALICE *exits, banging the door behind her*) I knew that would annoy her!
(*She chuckles*)

XENIA She got out of bed with the left foot, this morning.

JUNE Her behavior recently has left much to be desired. I may have to speak to her mother—

XENIA She has her mother here?

JUNE In Glasgow. Inoffensive old soul. Bakes cakes;

minds her own business, but a terrific mumbler. Can't understand a word she says.

(*She essays a few words of high-pitched, vaguely Scottish-sounding gibberish*)

XENIA   Oh, you are a scream!

JUNE   Well, come on—let's open the Champers. (*Looks at the flowers*) Then we can clear out all the foliage . . .
(*The doorbell rings*)

XENIA   I go. Soon we shall need a greenhouse.

JUNE   It's awfully kind of you to help out today.

XENIA   My darling: for you I do anything. (*The doorbell rings*) Perhaps this one is from Buckingham Palace?

JUNE   And about time too, they've been slacking!
(*JUNE opens the champagne*)

XENIA (*Off*)   Did you want to see Miss Buckridge?

JUNE   Now then—
(*The cork pops from the bottle*)

MRS. MERCY (*Enters. She is dressed in mourning, with a small veiled hat*)   I do hope I'm not disturbing you.

JUNE (*Surprised*)   Mrs. Mercy! No, of course not . . .

MRS. MERCY (*Handing over a bouquet*)   Dear Sister George—for you—a little tribute—from all of us in ad-min. at BH.

JUNE (*Nonplussed*)   Oh. Thanks. Extremely decent of you. I—appreciate the thought. Would you be an angel, Madame, and put them in water? Oh, I'm terribly sorry:

93

do you know each other? This is Madame Xenia—Mrs. Mercy Croft.

XENIA (*Bearing down on* MRS. MERCY) What, *the* Mrs. Mercy?

JUNE Of course, didn't you know—

XENIA (*Softly to* MRS. MERCY) But I love you, my dear. (*Shouting*) I *adore* you!

MRS. MERCY Have I had the pleasure?

XENIA You don't know me from Adam, my darling, but for twenty years I have listened to you—every single week!

JUNE How nice.

MRS. MERCY Charming!

XENIA (*Quite overcome*) I am—I cannot tell you—your advice is a hundred per cent. A hundred and twenty per cent! One senses—you have a heart, you have suffered—

MRS. MERCY Well, we all have our ups and downs.

XENIA But you have had more downs than ups—am I right?

MRS. MERCY I shouldn't like—

XENIA Of course I am! I knew it at once! Ask George here: am I ever wrong?

JUNE Never. She is quite infallible. You see, Madame Xenia is a clairvoyant.

MRS. MERCY Oh, really.

94

XENIA A psychometrist.

JUNE Oh, sorry.

XENIA I write a syndicated column every week: star fore-casts—hack work, but what-the-hell, one's got to live.

MRS. MERCY I'm afraid I don't really believe in that kind of—

XENIA (*Quickly*) Be careful what you do on the tenth. There's treachery around you. Don't sign any important documents before full moon—

MRS. MERCY I'm obliged to you, but really—

XENIA There's news from abroad—

MRS. MERCY (*Turning to* JUNE) I thought you'd be all alone this morning. That's why I came—

JUNE Very kind of you.

XENIA You're inclined to suffer from digestive disorders. Don't worry, it's nothing serious—

JUNE (*Apologetically*) Madame is helping me out today.

XENIA A tall man doesn't like you. Avoid him.

MRS. MERCY It would be somewhat difficult in my job to—

XENIA An old association will be broken. Never mind: there are plenty of birds in the sky—

MRS. MERCY (*Icily*) I think you mean fish in the sea.

XENIA (*To herself*) Interesting. Must be born under

95

Pisces . . . (*Cheerfully*) Oh well, I'll get some water for
the flowers . . .
(*She exits*)

JUNE She's been frightfully good: done all the organizing for me today.

MRS. MERCY Isn't your friend—er—Miss—?

JUNE Miss McNaught? She's not up yet! I'm afraid she's
no good at times like these. No backbone. Ballast.

MRS. MERCY (*Inspecting the wreaths*) What beautiful
tributes! May I read some? I *adore* inscriptions.

JUNE There's a whole lot more in the bathroom. As soon
as Childie's dressed she can take the whole damn lot
and dump them on the Cenotaph.

MRS. MERCY But you can't do that! They're for *you*.
(*Seriously*) Do you know the entire Applehurst Company turned up for the recording today in black? It was
quite spontaneous.

JUNE (*Annoyed*) They must be bonkers! I can just see
old Mrs. Hinch. She must have looked like The Phantom
of the Opera . . . (*Sees* MRS. MERCY's *black suit*) Oh,
I beg your pardon.

MRS. MERCY We felt we couldn't let her go without some
mark of respect. After all, she has been with us . . .
how long?

JUNE Six perishing years.

MRS. MERCY Oh, come now—you know you enjoyed every
minute of it.

JUNE (*Getting exasperated*) Yes, but it's over—I just want to forget it—

MRS. MERCY I don't think your public will let you. (*Indicates the wreaths*) You can see how much you meant to them.

JUNE (*Trying to escape*) Actually, I was just on the point of changing . . .
(*Takes off hat*)

MRS. MERCY For the funeral?

JUNE For the broadcast.
(MADAME XENIA *re-enters, brandishing a large gilded vase in the shape of a galleon bearing* MRS. MERCY's *flowers*)

XENIA All right?

JUNE Wasn't there something a little more conservative?

XENIA I can put them in a milk bottle, if you like. Or perhaps you'd prefer a bottle of gin? (*Piqued*) It is good to have one's hard work appreciated! Getting up early in the morning—

JUNE Madame, darling—I'm eternally grateful. You've been a brick!

XENIA Yes, so I've been told before.

MRS. MERCY What a charming message. (*Reading*)
"Ever-present, spirit-like,
Harken! the familiar sound:
Sister George, astride her bike,
In the happy hunting ground."
(JUNE *mutters under her breath*)

XENIA (*About to go*) Well, happy hunting, Sister George!

97

JUNE   You're off then, are you, dear?

XENIA   I'm afraid my client is waiting. The moment you need me, just stamp on the floor.

JUNE   Don't worry about me—I'm feeling fine. If any more flowers come, you'd better shove them in the coalshed.

XENIA   Leave everything to me. *I am your friend!*

MRS. MERCY   (*Reading*)   "Fare thee well. Go in peace, good woman."

XENIA   I can take a hint.
         (*She strides out, nose in the air*)

JUNE   (*Blowing her a kiss*)   Thank you, darling.

MRS. MERCY   You do have a lot of friends, don't you?

JUNE   I hope so. I like to think—

MRS. MERCY   Loneliness is the great scourge of our time.

JUNE   Too true.

MRS. MERCY   I had visions of you, sitting by your set, alone with your grief . . .

JUNE   With Miss McNaught actually, but it comes to the same thing.

MRS. MERCY   Frankly, I'm amazed you're taking it like this.

JUNE   Like what?

MRS. MERCY   So calmly. Cheerfully.

98

JUNE The uncertainty was the worst. Once that was over . . .

MRS. MERCY You have a very strong character. (*After a pause*) Will you go on listening to the program now?

JUNE I don't know. I hadn't really thought. Probably not. I mean—it might be rather—distressing—listening to all the old voices going on without me . . .

MRS. MERCY Isn't that a rather selfish attitude to take?

JUNE Selfish?

MRS. MERCY You died to save the series—surely you'll want to take an interest in its fortunes?

JUNE Well . . .

MRS. MERCY I think the next few episodes will be particularly fascinating. (*She warms to the subject*) Your death means an enormous re-adjustment to the whole community. It will take them weeks, even months, to get over the shock. But eventually the gap must be filled, new leaders will arise—

JUNE Leaders? What leaders? Who?

MRS. MERCY (*Confidentially*) Well, it's not really for release yet, but between you and me—I believe Ginger—

JUNE (*Horrified*) Ginger? (*Slipping into country accent*) He couldn't lead a cow down Buttercup Hill. He's weak! Weak as rotten apples dropping off a tree.

MRS. MERCY Ginger will be our anti-hero.

JUNE An anti-hero in Applehurst?

MRS. MERCY   Contemporary appeal. Applehurst is facing up to the fact that the old values have become outdated.

JUNE   I wonder how old Mrs. Hinch is going to take that?

MRS. MERCY   (*Quickly*)   Not very well, I'm afraid. She passes away.

JUNE   (*Aghast*)   *What!*

MRS. MERCY   It's due in the second week in December.

JUNE   How?

MRS. MERCY   It'll be a cold winter in Applehurst. She gets up in the middle of the night to let the cat in . . .

JUNE   And—?

MRS. MERCY   Bronchitis. Gone in two days.

JUNE   But you can't do this! After all the care I gave that woman—why, I've nursed her from gout to gastro-enteritis over the last six years.

MRS. MERCY   That's neither here nor there.

JUNE   I could have saved her—just as I saved old Mr. Burns last winter. He's three years older and look at him now, fit as a fiddle! At least he was . . .

MRS. MERCY   I'm afraid he is due for a stroke next Friday.

JUNE   But why all this carnage, all this slaughter?

MRS. MERCY   We live in a violent world, Miss Buckridge, surrounded by death and destruction. It's the policy of the BBC to face up to reality.

JUNE   Who's going to look after the survivors?

MRS. MERCY   Nurse Lawrence.

JUNE   What!

MRS. MERCY   Yes, she arrives from the District Hospital tomorrow to take over from you.

JUNE   But she's a probationer. She couldn't put a dressing on a salad! They won't stand for that, you know.

MRS. MERCY   On the contrary, Nurse Lawrence wins the trust and affection of the village, and becomes known, rather charmingly, I think, as Sister Larry.

JUNE   (*Rising*)   You're going to make this ill-bred, uneducated slut—

MRS. MERCY   (*Shouting*)   Contemporary appeal, Sister George! People like that *do* exist—and in positions of power and influence; flawed, credible characters like Ginger, Nurse Lawrence, Rosie—

JUNE   What about Rosie?

MRS. MERCY   She's pregnant.

JUNE   I know that. And as she's not married, that's about as flawed and credible as you can get!

MRS. MERCY   She's going to marry her boy friend, Lennie.

JUNE   Oh good. I'm glad . . . I'm glad about that . . . glad—

MRS. MERCY   Mind you, it's not his baby.

JUNE   Eh?

MRS. MERCY   It's Roy's from the army camp at Oakmead. She tells Lennie, makes a full confession, and he forgives her, and they live happily ever after.

101

JUNE Pardon me while I vomit.

ALICE (*Enters. She is wearing a gaily colored dress*) Oh, hello.

MRS. MERCY (*Cordially*) Hello, dear. I was wondering where you were.

ALICE I didn't go to work today.

MRS. MERCY No, of course not.

ALICE (*Sweetly, to* MRS. MERCY) Can I make you a cup of tea, Mrs. Mercy?

MRS. MERCY I'd *adore* a cup of tea!

JUNE (*Bitterly*) Mrs. Mercy came over to bring me the good news that I'm to be replaced by Nurse Lawrence.

ALICE Nurse Lawrence—Nurse Lawrence? Do I know her?

JUNE Don't be irritating. Of course you know her. That interfering busybody from Oakmead—

ALICE (*With indifference*) Oh, her.

JUNE Yes, her.

ALICE (*To* JUNE) Anyway, it's not really your concern any more what happens in Applehurst. You're out of it—

JUNE (*Bellowing*) Don't you understand? Don't you understand anything? I built it up: I made it what it is! It's not *nice* to see one's life work ruined!

MRS. MERCY I have one piece of cheering news for you, if you can bear to hear it.

JUNE   I can bear it. Pour out a glass of gin for me, Childie, while you're over at the sideboard. Sorry, Mrs. Mercy, you were saying . . .

MRS. MERCY   It concerns your future.

JUNE   My future, yes. You are quite right: we must talk of the future. Is there still time—?

MRS. MERCY   There's still nearly an hour to go.

JUNE   Did you want to stay for the . . . the . . .

MRS. MERCY   Broadcast?

JUNE   The funeral. Yes . . .

MRS. MERCY   No, I'll have to get back to BH. We're having a little party, you know. Perhaps "party" isn't quite the right word.

ALICE   A wake?

MRS. MERCY   I suppose one could call it that. That's why I want a quick word with you, Miss Buckridge. Mrs. Coote has promised to come. You know Mrs. Coote, don't you? She's in charge of Toddler Time.

JUNE   Yes, of course I know her, a charming woman.

MRS. MERCY   Well, dear, she's very anxious to have you.

JUNE   Really?

MRS. MERCY   What I'm telling you now is strictly off the cuff. Everything's still in the planning stage. I thought I'd nip over and tell you that there's a ray of sunshine on the horizon.

JUNE   I'm all ears.
   (ALICE *exits to the kitchen*)

MRS. MERCY (*Very confidentially*)   Well, dear, as you probably know, Toddler Time has been—what shall we say—a wee bit disappointing. Audience research figures —this is strictly *entre nous*, you understand—

JUNE   Yes, yes of course.

MRS. MERCY   —show a slight but perceptible slide. Mrs. Coote, I may tell you, is worried out of her mind! She hasn't slept a wink for three weeks—

JUNE   Poor love!

MRS. MERCY   The scriptwriters are running around in circles—one of them's had a nervous breakdown: the one who wrote that series about Tiddlywink, the Cockerel, which, as you know, was taken off after only three installments. Anyway, to cut a long story short, there's been some agonizing reappraisal over Toddler Time. A completely new approach has been decided on—

JUNE   Don't tell me—marauding gollywogs, drunk teddybears and pregnant bunnies!
   (ALICE *re-enters with tea*)

MRS. MERCY (*Smiling enigmatically*)   Not quite, dear. But we're preparing an absolutely super adventure serial, in which we've got loads of confidence, which will combine exciting narrative with a modern outlook. And you're being considered for the title role.

JUNE   What is it called?

MRS. MERCY   The World of Clarabelle Cow.

104

Beryl Reid as SISTER GEORGE, Eileen Atkins as ALICE "CHILDIE"
MCNAUGHT and Lally Bowers as MRS. MERCY CROFT

JUNE (*Rising after a pause*) Am I to understand that this . . . this character is a cow?

MRS. MERCY A very human one, I assure you: full of little foibles and prejudices—

JUNE (*Slowly*) A . . . flawed . . . credible . . . cow?

MRS. MERCY Credible in human terms, certainly. Otherwise the children wouldn't believe in her. Children are very discerning!

ALICE Ought to be fun.

JUNE I don't think I could have understood you correctly. I don't believe I really grasped the meaning of your words.

MRS. MERCY I thought I made myself perfectly clear.

ALICE Oh, don't be dense, George!

JUNE (*To* ALICE) Be quiet! (*To* MRS. MERCY) Am I to take it that you have come here today—the day of the funeral of Sister George—to offer me the part of a cow?

MRS. MERCY We've got to be practical, dear. None of us can afford to be out of work for too long.

JUNE Childie, give me another gin! (*To* MRS. MERCY) You're not serious, are you? You're joking, aren't you?

MRS. MERCY We don't joke about these things at the BBC, Miss Buckridge.

ALICE (*To* JUNE) It's jolly nice of Mrs. Mercy to come over specially to tell you.

MRS. MERCY I thought it was a brilliant idea of Mrs. Coote's.

JUNE (*Shouting and tearing her hair*) I can't stand it! I'm going mad!

XENIA (*Enters with another wreath*) One more for luck!

JUNE (*Tonelessly*) From whom?

XENIA (*Reading the inscription*) "I never thought I'd survive you. Signed: Mrs. Ethel Hinch."

MRS. MERCY She doesn't know yet . . .

JUNE (*Distracted*) She's going to die, Madame Xenia— in two months' time! They're going to murder her, too. An old lady of eighty-five, who's never done anyone the slightest harm!

XENIA How terrible! Are you sure?

JUNE (*Wildly to* MRS. MERCY) Murderess!
    (*She lunges at* MRS. MERCY *and is held back by* ALICE *and* MADAME XENIA)

MRS. MERCY Really, Miss Buckridge! Restrain yourself!

JUNE Is your blood lust sated? How many other victims are you going to claim?

MRS. MERCY (*Shrilly*) Control yourself!

ALICE George, you're drunk!

XENIA My darling is upset. She's had a shock.

JUNE (*Making a great effort to control herself*) With reference to Toddler Time, please thank Mrs. Coote for her kind interest—

MRS. MERCY There's no need for you to decide today—

JUNE —and tell her I cannot possibly accept the part in question.

MRS. MERCY Very well, I'll tell her.
    (*The buzzer sounds*)

ALICE Don't be silly, George. You can't afford to turn down—

JUNE I'm not playing the part of a cow!

XENIA A cow? What cow?

JUNE (*Frantically*) I'M NOT PLAYING THE PART OF A COW ! !

MRS. MERCY I've taken your point, Miss Buckridge!

XENIA . . . There are two nuns, to see Sister George.

JUNE No! . . . NO ! !
    (*Groaning with dismay, she rushes off to the bathroom*)

XENIA (*To* MRS. MERCY) Nuns before noon is a good omen!

MRS. MERCY I'll take your word for it.

ALICE (*Following* JUNE) I'd better go and see what she's doing. (*Goes to the bathroom. Off-stage*) . . . George: what are you doing?

XENIA (*Into the speaker*) I'm sorry, Sister George is getting ready for her funeral.

ALICE (*Long pause*) George! . . . (*She re-enters*) She appears to be running a bath.

XENIA Shall I go and speak to her?

MRS. MERCY She won't do anything silly, will she?

XENIA (*To* ALICE) See if she's all right! (ALICE *goes off again*) I'm so worried.

MRS. MERCY There was bound to be a reaction.

ALICE (*Off-stage*) George? . . . I can't hear what you're saying! Turn the bloody taps off!
(JUNE *mumbles off-stage*)

XENIA Oi, oi, oi.

ALICE (*Re-entering*) Says she wants to be left alone.

XENIA How did she sound?

ALICE Like a walrus.

XENIA (*Clapping her hands*) Thank God. Thank God she's herself again. (*Tidying up confusedly*) Oi, oi, what a morning!
(*She exits.* MRS. MERCY *and* ALICE *face each other for a few seconds. Then* MRS. MERCY *extends her arms, and* ALICE *flies to her, and bursts into tears*)

MRS. MERCY My poor child . . . There, there . . .

ALICE I can't stand it any more.

MRS. MERCY I know, dear, I know. You've been under a terrible strain.

ALICE You've no idea, Mrs. Mercy—

MRS. MERCY I can imagine.

ALICE She's been *terrible*!

MRS. MERCY Hush, dear. She'll hear you.

ALICE I was praying you'd come.

MRS. MERCY I wasn't going to leave you alone with her today. (*She smiles*) Besides, I had promised.

ALICE Oh, I know, but I knew how busy you were.

MRS. MERCY First things first.

ALICE I knew I could rely on you. I felt it the first time I met you.

MRS. MERCY And I felt that I was speaking to a proud and sensitive person, whose personality was being systematically crushed.

ALICE Don't!

MRS. MERCY And with a definite literary talent.

ALICE Honestly? Do you really think so?

MRS. MERCY I'm being quite objective.

ALICE Gosh. Wouldn't it be marvelous?

MRS. MERCY What, dear?

ALICE If I could do some work for you—writing, I mean.

MRS. MERCY We shall see what transpires. I'll certainly give you all the help I can.

ALICE Oh, you are nice!

MRS. MERCY And the other offer still stands.

ALICE Yes, well . . . I think I've almost definitely decided. I'm sorry to be so vague . . .

MRS. MERCY Not at all.

ALICE It's a bit of wrench, you know. I've been working for Mr. Katz for nearly four years. I'd have to give him a month's notice—

MRS. MERCY There's no rush. I told you I'd keep the job open for a fortnight.

ALICE And there's George.

MRS. MERCY Yes.

ALICE I mean: I don't know how she'd take it.

MRS. MERCY You haven't told her, of course?

ALICE God, no. She'd have murdered me!

MRS. MERCY In view of what happened today, I think we were very wise—

ALICE If she suspected I'd been to see you behind her back—

MRS. MERCY But there was no reason why you shouldn't. You're perfectly entitled—

ALICE Oh, I *know*. But she's so possessive. She never allows me anywhere near the BBC. I'm kept a guilty secret.

MRS. MERCY She's shackled you to her. Anyway, you wouldn't be working for the BBC: you'd be working as my own private secretary, in my London flat.

ALICE   It sounds absolutely super. I'm sorry I'm being so slow about making up my mind.

MRS. MERCY   A thought has just occurred to me: if you're in any kind of trouble—you know, with George—you can always camp down at the flat. There's a divan—

ALICE   Oh, that'd be *wonderful!*

MRS. MERCY   It could serve as your temporary HQ. It's not luxurious, mind you.

ALICE   Never mind that. It would be an escape . . . if necessary . . .

MRS. MERCY   That's what I thought. I only ever stay there if I've been kept late at a story conference, or something like that. I find it useful . . . I suppose it's really a place to escape for me, too . . .

ALICE   We'd be like prisoners on the run . . .

MRS. MERCY   Do you really think you can escape?

ALICE   (*After a pause*)   I don't know.

MRS. MERCY   It's very difficult for you.

ALICE   It's been so long, so many years . . .

MRS. MERCY   It's hard to break the routine.

ALICE   It's little things one misses most.

MRS. MERCY   (*Smiling*)   You could bring your dolls.

ALICE   (*Grabbing Emmeline*)   I couldn't go anywhere without them. I even take them on holiday—and then

I'm terrified they'll get lost or stolen. Sometimes George hides them—it's her idea of a joke . . .

MRS. MERCY   A very cruel joke.

ALICE (*Clutching* MRS. MERCY)   Don't let her get at me, Mrs. Mercy! Stay here—don't go away!

MRS. MERCY   I can't stay here all day, dear.

ALICE   Don't leave me alone—I'm frightened of what she will do!

MRS. MERCY   Calm yourself, Alice. No one's going to hurt you. Here, put your head on my shoulder; close your eyes . . . Relax—my goodness, you're trembling like a leaf . . .
(*She strokes* ALICE's *hair*)

ALICE   That's nice . . .

MRS. MERCY   You're my little girl. You're going to be . . . my little girl . . .

JUNE (*Enters. She is wearing her bath robe*)   What a touching sight . . .

ALICE (*Panic-stricken, breaking away from* MRS. MERCY)   George!

JUNE (*To* MRS. MERCY)   I always did say she had nice hair. That's one thing I always said for her . . .

ALICE   George, you don't understand!

JUNE (*Grabbing the doll*)   Your mummy says I don't understand. Did you see what your mummy was doing with that strange lady?

MRS. MERCY She was overwrought, Miss Buckridge. I tried to comfort her.

JUNE How absolutely sweet of you! And how well you have succeeded!
  (ALICE *is trembling from head to toe*)

MRS. MERCY I hope you don't think—

JUNE (*Sweetly*) Alice, Childie: come here a minute. I want to say something to you! . . . (ALICE *looks terrified*) Come along, don't be frightened, I'm not going to hurt you.

ALICE Why can't you tell me—in front of Mrs. Mercy?

JUNE (*Feigning gaucheness*) Well, you know, boy's talk—

MRS. MERCY Would you rather I left?

JUNE Oh no, no. Whatever could have given you that idea? Come along, keep still. I only want to whisper it in your ear.
  (*She whispers something*)

ALICE (*Shouting*) No! (JUNE *whispers something else*) No, I'm not going to do it!

JUNE Yes or no, Childie? Yes or no?

ALICE (*Frantically*) No, no, NO!

MRS. MERCY (*White with indignation*) What are you asking her to do, Sister George?

JUNE The appropriate treatment, that's all. The punishment that fits the crime . . .

113

ALICE (*Shrieking*)　She wants me to drink her bath water!

MRS. MERCY (*Astounded*)　Her bath water?

ALICE　To humiliate me!

MRS. MERCY (*Rising*)　But this is preposterous! I've never heard of such an obscene suggestion!

JUNE　You're shut off from the world, Mrs. Mercy! "Ask Mrs. Mercy"—all your problems answered! "Dear Mrs. Mercy, what shall I do? My flatmate is nasty to me and wants me to drink her bath water. By the time you reply to me—glug, glug, glug—it may be too late—glug—and I might have drowned!"

MRS. MERCY (*To* ALICE)　I strongly advise you to leave this house at once!

JUNE (*To* ALICE)　Well, you have had the benefit of Mrs. Mercy's expert advice. Are you going to take it?

ALICE　I'm sorry, George, I can't stay with you any longer.

MRS. MERCY　Very sensible.

JUNE　Did you hear what your mummy said, Emmeline? Your mummy wants to leave us—

MRS. MERCY　I wish you wouldn't—

JUNE (*Dangerously*)　Mind what you're saying, Mrs. Mercy: this is between Alice and myself!

ALICE (*Pleading*)　Let me have Emmeline!

JUNE　Glug, glug, glug to you.
　　　(*She makes the doll point at* MRS. MERCY)

MRS. MERCY   I don't know how you can be so cruel. The poor child—

JUNE   "The poor child!" As you're going to see quite a lot of "the poor child," I'd better put you in the picture about her—

ALICE   George, don't! George, please!

JUNE   "The poor child" likes to pretend she's a baby, but take a close look at her!
(ALICE *bursts into tears*)

MRS. MERCY   Can't you see you're upsetting the child!

JUNE (*Shouting*)   The child? The child is a woman— she's thirty-four! (*A loud sob from* ALICE) She's old enough to have a grandchild!

MRS. MERCY   Oh, really, now you're exaggerating—

JUNE   Am I? *Am I?*

ALICE (*Whimpering*)   Don't, George . . . don't . . .

JUNE (*With disgust*)   Look at you: whimpering and pleading! Have you no backbone, can't you stand up like a man—

ALICE (*Sobbing*)   I can't . . . help it . . .

JUNE   "I can't help it!" She'll never change—feckless, self-indulgent—

ALICE   I'm going! I'm packing my bag!
(*She runs to the door, but* JUNE *bars the way*)

JUNE   Come back here!

MRS. MERCY   Let her go! Let her go!

JUNE (*To* MRS. MERCY) You've got yourself a prize packet there, I can tell you!

ALICE (*Screaming*) Let me go!

JUNE She had an illegitimate child when she was eighteen. She gave it away—to strangers! She has a daughter of sixteen . . . (ALICE *collapses on the floor in a heap*) Do what you like—you make me sick!
(*She sits in an armchair*)

MRS. MERCY Stop crying, dear. Go and pack, quickly. You needn't take everything now. Go along, hurry! I'll wait for you here . . .
(ALICE *goes into the bedroom*)

MRS. MERCY I'm sorry Miss Buckridge, about all this. It'll be all for the best, you'll see . . . I do hope you're not bearing me any grudge—(JUNE *shakes her head*) Oh, good, good. Sometimes it's best to make a clean break— it's painful, but that's the advice I always give in my program. Which reminds me: it's almost time for the broadcast. Shall I switch it on? (*She switches on the radio*) Let it give you strength, Miss Buckridge. Remember: Sister George was not killed because she was hated, but because she was loved! (ALICE *comes on, tear-stained, carrying a small case*) If you study anthropology, you'll discover that in primitive societies it was always the best-loved member of the community who was selected as the sacrificial victim. By killing him they hoped that the goodness and strength of the victim would pass on to them. It was both a purge and a rededication. What you will hear in a few moments is the purge and rededication of Applehurst. Good-bye, Sister George.
(*From the radio comes the slow tolling of a bell*)

ALICE I think she's right in what she said: Mrs. Mercy, I mean. I love you, too, George, that's why I've got to leave you. You do understand, don't you . . . I mean— (*She's starting to cry again*) All right, Mrs. Mercy, I'm coming. Good-bye, George, and—you know—thanks for everything!

    (ALICE *and* MRS. MERCY *exit*)

ANNOUNCER'S VOICE: (*From the radio*) Applehurst: a chronicle of an English village. This is a sad day for Applehurst. The church bell is tolling for the funeral of Sister George, the well-beloved District Nurse, whose forthright, practical, no-nonsense manner had endeared her to the community. But death comes to the best of us, and the picturesque village is today swathed in mourning . . .

    (*The church bell tolls again*)

JUNE (*A very plaintive sound*) Moo! . . . (*Louder*) Moo! Moo!

    (*A heart-rending sound*)
                      Curtain